John F. Kennedy

AND A NEW GENERATION

David Burner

John F. Kennedy

AND A NEW GENERATION

Edited by Oscar Handlin

LITTLE, BROWN AND COMPANY
BOSTON   **TORONTO**   **LONDON**

Copyright © 1988 by David Burner

Acknowledgments

From Robert Frost, "For John F. Kennedy on His Inaguration" from *The Poetry of Robert Frost* edited by Edward Connery Lathem. Copyright © 1961 by Robert Frost. Reprinted by permission of Henry Holt and Company, the Estate of Robert Frost, and Jonathan Cape Ltd.

Excerpt from *The New York Times* (1957). Copyright © 1957 by The New York Times Company. Reprinted by permission.

Excerpt from *The New York Times* (1963). Copyright © 1963 by The New York Times Company. Reprinted by permission.

Library of Congress Cataloging-in-Publication Data

Burner, David, 1937–
    John F. Kennedy and a new generation / David Burner; edited by Oscar Handlin.
        p.   cm. — (The Library of American biography)
    Bibliography: p.
    Includes index.
    ISBN 0-316-11724-2
    1. Kennedy, John F. (John Fitzgerald), 1917–1963. 2. Presidents— United States—Biography. 3. United States—Politics and government—1961–1963. I. Handlin, Oscar, 1915– . II. Title. III. Series.
E842.B79 1988b
973.922′092′4—dc19   88-15595
[B]   CIP

10 9 8 7 6 5 4 3 2 1

BP

Published simultaneously in Canada
by Little, Brown & Company (Canada) Limited

Printed in the United States of America

for Sandy

Editor's Preface

FOR A FEW days in November 1963, the nation focused on an event that began with the assassination in Dallas and ended with the state funeral in Washington. The murder of John F. Kennedy, captured on film and endlessly replayed; the dramatic aftermath, in which his killer was gunned down within sight of the television cameras; and the somber procession to the burial place; all evoked an uncommon depth of grief that united the whole country.

The president had been far from the peak of his popularity in that year and he faced many unsolved problems before the election twelve months ahead. But the country forgot those doubts and invested him with a martyr's image that expressed its own wish for unity. The unexpected, utterly capricious act seemed to symbolize the uncertainties in contemporary life.

It also left hopes unfulfilled. Few then knew the complications already beginning to unfold at home and abroad, but many were aware that the expectations raised three years earlier had not produced the expected fruit.

Some citizens thought back to the inauguration. On a wintry Washington day the new young president spoke among the snowflakes, summoning his countrymen to meet unavoidable challenges. "Ask not what your country can do for you; ask what you can do for your country." He himself was hardly aware of the words' full meaning. In the years that followed the slogans resonated—New Frontier, Alliance for Progress, A New Generation. They summoned up visions of youthful vibrancy and strength, in contrast to the administration of the aging president then leaving office.

The actuality was different, and our author examines the contrast. John F. Kennedy, youthful in reality and in appearance, was hardly one of the people. He sprang from a distinctive upper class that combined a background of wealth, Harvard education, and affiliations with a Boston Irish clan that followed its own rules. He came into office confident that he could draw upon the country's brightest and best talents to break through the encrusted habits of the preceding years. Not always visible, but behind him, was a powerful, domineering father. The interplay among these influences shaped the response to grave domestic and diplomatic problems, and furnishes the dramatic stuff of a story interesting in itself and illuminating United States development in the crucial years after 1960.

OSCAR HANDLIN

Contents

John F. Kennedy

AND A NEW GENERATION

I

Being a Kennedy

DURING THE SUMMER OF 1960, some college freshmen were asked to tell whom they would prefer to see elected President of the United States, John F. Kennedy or Richard M. Nixon, the candidates that year, and why. A young Chinese student responded "John F. Ken . . . because he makes me feel I am an American." People of various backgrounds who were then not entirely comfortable with their American identities have similar memories of the brief incandescent Kennedy presidential years. Perhaps in the light of history, the enduring glow of John Fitzgerald Kennedy's name arises most elementally from his outsider status as a Roman Catholic anointed to the highest office in the land. In a moment Kennedy had broken the iron tradition restricting the White House to Protestants. That election night in 1960 has powerful meaning not only for fellow Catholics of various ethnic strains but also for other minority groups: Jews, blacks, Hispanics, and Asians. Kennedy's achievement represents a partial fulfillment of a national promise that Americans even of recent immigrant background might reach for wealth, homes, education for their children, or an ideal of justice.

More than a century ago these dreams were nourished in Ireland, a country that in the 1840s was probably more impoverished than any other in Europe. In Ireland landlords exported grain in spite of domestic want. Although Jack Kennedy's ancestors were not among the poorest of the Irish, they suffered deeply when a fungus brought from America turned three successive crops of potatoes black and putrid. As a result

1

of the crop failures, a quarter of the population fled starvation in fetid holds of ships destined for Boston. Among these immigrants were Jack Kennedy's first American paternal relatives, Patrick Kennedy and his wife Bridget Murphy, who arrived together in Boston early in 1849, lucky to be alive after their perilous Atlantic crossing. They lived in corrugated shacks on Noddle's Island in Boston harbor until they were married later that year. Patrick began work as a cooper, laboring daily with the adze and croze to bend wooden staves into barrels or the familiar yokes of Conestoga wagons. He died in his early thirties, probably of cholera or consumption, soon after fathering a son. Patrick's early death was not unusual in this city where on average the immigrant survived for only fourteen years; the mortality rate of the Boston poor was higher than that of the poor of any major European city. The Boston Irish lived under grim conditions in the first major immigrant ghetto in America. Even Massachusetts abolitionists who pitied slaves in the South felt scarcely a twang of conscience over living conditions right in their midst.

Yet the Irish heritage offered the immigrants some defenses against the impersonality of the dominant laissez-faire economics that postulated a world of coldly separate individuals. While the Irish favored strong individualism, they practiced it in a communal setting. Conditions in Ireland had produced invisible loyalties based on common memories and myths. On their own soil the Irish had long fought and bargained locally with the governing British, confronting higher authority somewhat as ethnic groups in the United States learned to deal with the rest of the American polity. Their church, their secret societies, and their Catholic Association movement provided them with an organization and a national political identity. In Boston the Irish immigrants congregated in neighborhoods, took part in church rituals, gathered in saloons, and formed political clubs. Their political participation would give them a voice in America.

That political philosophy, however, was not necessarily liberal. Irish-Americans opposed the antislavery movement, women's rights, and public schools. By the twentieth century the Irish in some cities had acquired a vigorous political record on tangible issues such as better wages, shorter working hours, and safer factory conditions. But since the motive behind those politics is the wish to defend the home, family, and neighborhood, the apparent progressivism is at the same time a social conservatism. Among many twentieth-century ethnic Irish, fidelity to these good traditional institutions has blended with a visceral red-baiting and racism.

The widowed mother of the American-born Patrick ("P. J.") Kennedy squeezed out a living running a notions shop. The young Patrick dropped out of school and worked for some time as a stevedore. Later, after having become proprietor of a neighborhood saloon that he had financed from his own and his mother's savings, he chose politics as a second career. His tactics of dispensing advice and friendship to those in need and of giving free beer to voters enabled him to enter the Massachusetts state senate. Soon he was importing Haig & Haig Scotch, selling it to Boston's better hotels and restaurants. In 1888 he seconded Grover Cleveland's nomination for the presidency of the United States. Nicknamed the "Mayor of East Boston" and known as one of the city's four most influential politicians behind the scenes, Patrick Kennedy later earned his living both as a liquor wholesaler and as a banker. His marriage to Mary Hickey, the sister of the mayor of Brockton, benefited his social and economic status. Although Patrick and Mary played classical music and a daughter has described her father as idealistic and her mother as visionary, they still maintained an insular, provincial life on the islands in the harbor that made up East Boston. Boston's politics were now, for better or worse and doubtless for both, largely dominated by the Irish, and one of P.J.'s descendants would eventually rise on that base to leadership of his country. It was not, however, a politics controlled by a single machine like a Tammany Hall. Individual clan chieftains such as Martin Lomasney, Daniel Coakley, James Michael Curley, and John Francis Fitzgerald used ruthless tactics to keep their supporters in line, and John F. Kennedy's father and grandfather laid claim to an area in Massachusetts comprising parts of Cambridge, Brighton, and Waltham that ultimately provided JFK with a congressional seat.

P.J.'s son, Joseph Patrick Kennedy (1888-1969), began his progress out of the Irish ghetto into the wider worlds of business, politics, and diplomacy when his parents transferred him from East Boston's Xaverian school to the famous Boston Latin School. This was a clear if unintentional exodus from a community indrawn and carefully guarded by such injunctions as Archbishop William O'Connell's frequent warning to the faithful not to send their children to Protestant schools. Both as a boy and as a man the young Joe Kennedy steadily pursued wealth. "How can we make some money?" was a characteristic childhood greeting. Like Al Smith, he hawked newspapers on the urban sidewalks, becoming streetwise and meeting pimps, prostitutes, and racketeers. As captain of his parochial school's baseball team, the Assumptions, Joe used his earnings to buy eye-catching baseball uniforms and took on a genteel team, the Playfairs, whom his boys thrashed. In college Joe earned some $10,000 by operating a sightseeing bus line through the older sections of Boston.

At Boston Latin the good-looking gregarious Joe prepared for Harvard. An inattentive student, Joe took an extra year to earn his diploma, playing baseball and football, managing the basketball team, commanding a drill regiment, and getting elected class president. The school yearbook predicted that he would make his mark "in a very roundabout way." Harvard accepted him as until the 1950s it did practically any scion of a successful family. At Harvard Joe switched from the difficult study of economics to the less demanding field of music. He kept his love for classical music nearly hidden: it might appear not quite "muscular" enough for a practical businessman and politician. He rarely read a book, either in college or in later life. Though successful in athletics and in making friends, Joe was denied membership in the best Harvard social clubs. Some thought this exclusion to be because he was an Irish Catholic, but one Harvard faculty member recalls a different story: Joe was blackballed for his habitual lying.

Upon graduating, Joe chose banking as a quick route to attain his goal of becoming a millionaire by his mid-thirties. At first he rejected politics because he believed it would inevitably lead to defeat, as well as a dependency on a fickle public rather than on his own inner strength. As he later said to his wife, he wanted "the freedom which money provides, the freedom to come and go where he pleased, when he pleased and how he pleased." To learn the trade, he worked briefly at his father's East Boston Columbia Trust Company. Soon he became assistant bank examiner for the state "If you're going to get money," Kennedy explained, "you have to find out where it is." Within two years he borrowed to save Columbia Trust from a merger and to assume the presidency of the small bank. He claimed to be but was probably not the nation's youngest bank president. Joe Kennedy's political knowledge matured as he observed the effect of legislation on banks.

High ambition and zest for life led Joseph Kennedy to the doorstep of Rose Fitzgerald, daughter of Boston's colorful Mayor John Fitzgerald. Known as "Fitzie," and later as "Fitz" or the syrupy "Honey Fitz," his ancestry also reached back to County Wexford. That family, too, had Americanized itself. Rose's grandfather, John Francis Fitzgerald, the son of a peddler turned successful grocer, was born in 1863 in the North End of Boston, an immigrant district where three infants out of ten died before reaching the age of one. But John's parents prospered, and in 1879 they removed their newsboy son from the streets to Boston Latin School. Upon graduating he entered Harvard Medical School but left without a diploma when his father died. This act must have been a result of custom rather than need, for his father had left a considerable estate. John then apprenticed himself to a local boss whom he followed with absolute fidelity. In 1889 he married Mary Hannon, a quiet girl with a sunny disposition.

The Fitzgeralds' daughter Rose, born in 1890, was brought up as a member of the Irish upper classes. Placing third academically in her high school and being voted the prettiest senior, she entered the Convent of the Sacred Heart on Commonwealth Avenue in Boston. It had been her wish to attend Wellesley College, but Archbishop O'Connell persuaded her father not to send her to a secular college. "My greatest regret," she recalled, "is not having gone to Wellesley College. It is something I have felt a little sad about all my life." The next year her father, fearing political scandal after his first term as mayor, sent her to a Catholic finishing school at Blumenthal in Northern Germany. There she became accomplished in German and French and absorbed a curriculum of *Kinder, Kirche, Küche*—children, church, and cooking. The school was cold, and its discipline rigid. Every Sunday morning all the students gathered in the chapel for an evaluation of each girl's conduct, which included such faults as walking too fast or failing to curtsy before a religious statue. Rose may have lost a little of her spontaneity and independence at the German school, but after returning home, she ran charitable and social clubs at Manhattanville College (another branch of the Convent of the Sacred Heart), studied piano in Boston at the New England Conservatory of Music, participated in a little theater group, and became the youngest member of the Boston Public Library's book selection committee. She described herself as "the leader of the young Catholic set in Boston."

Honey Fitz enjoyed a long colorful career. He would sing "Sweet Adeline" at the slightest provocation. Once when a runaway truck ran him down after he had moved some children from its path, he would not let an ambulance take him to the hospital until he sat up and sang his trademark song to

reassure onlookers he was all right. When Franklin D. Roosevelt later sent him on a goodwill tour, Honey Fitz sang
"Dulce Adelina" from Colombia to Argentina. "He could talk
to you," according to an acquaintance's recollection, "for ten
or fifteen minutes at the rate of 200 words a minute, without
letting you get in more than two or three times, then pat you
on the back and tell you how much he enjoyed the conversation." Like other ethnic politicians of his day, Honey Fitz was
able to make city politics accessible to ordinary people in a way
that Brahmin bluebloods often could not. He had a "wake
squad" who, on his behalf, attended every wake in the city.
His victorious campaign for a second nonconsecutive mayoral
term charged his opponent with anti-Catholicism. Fitz has left
a reputation for taking graft and overloading the city payroll
with incompetent cronies while at the same time building
schools and hospitals in the slums; later he was removed from
Congress on charges of voting fraud.

Fitz allowed that Joe Kennedy's Harvard background and
bank presidency made him an acceptable suitor. Joe and Rose
were married in 1914, settling into a house in Protestant,
middle-class Brookline, Massachusetts. Joe's banking experience equipped him to be treasurer of Old Colony Realty,
which offered middle-class suburban sites to the new Irish,
where they would be safe from "the encroachment of unde-
sirable elements." It also bought up defaulted mortgages and
evicted poor Irish and Italian families before repainting and
reselling their homes. During World War I Joe served as assistant general manager of Bethlehem Steel's shipyards at
Quincy, earning $20,000 a year. Joe knew nothing of ship-
building but all about financing; he eventually developed an
ulcer while breaking production records, building thirty-six
destroyers in two years. When Kennedy refused to send two
frigates to Argentina without first getting paid for them, four
United States Navy tugs with armed servicemen towed the
boats away on the orders of Assistant Secretary of the Navy
Franklin D. Roosevelt. The two men thereby learned mutual

respect. Joe told his friend William Randolph Hearst that Roosevelt was even tougher than Joe was himself.

As the turn of the century was the age of the banker in the United States, the mid-1920s would be the start of the great bull market. In the twenties Joe learned almost all there was to know about manipulating the stock market, profiting heavily from insider trading. He believed that corporations existed for the benefit of the management, not the stockholders. But money, disappointing the American trust in it, does not quickly buy a place in patrician society. In the years when Kennedy was growing up, Boston newspapers carried one society section for the Irish and another for the Americans of older lineage. The Kennedys were not fully accepted socially either in the Protestant summer resort of Cohasset or later in Hyannis Port on Cape Cod, where the family sported a chauffeur-driven, plum-colored Rolls Royce. Kennedy was refused summer membership in the Cohasset Golf Club, and the Cape's season list of debutantes did not carry the names of his daughters. In 1926, while keeping his summer home on the Cape, Joe finally moved his rapidly growing family by private railroad car to Westchester County in New York—first, temporarily, to Riverdale and then to the restrictive community of Bronxville. The Kennedys were caught between classes; while they preferred not to associate with the lower-class Irish, many Yankees still snubbed them. A few years later Kennedy objected to a newspaper's calling him an Irish-American. Puzzled, he said, "I was born here. My children were born here. What the hell do I have to do to be an American?"

Leaving behind these class distinctions as well as his wife (after the last child was conceived in 1931 Rose declined for religious reasons to have sexual relations with him), Joe Kennedy went to Hollywood in the late 1920s. For some three years he participated in an industry that was bursting with sudden and freewheeling money-making as it catered to a demand of its own creation. Every week 60 million Americans went to the movies. Kennedy made some $6 million on cheaply made Tom Mix westerns and melodramas like *A Poor Girl's Romance* and *Red Hot Hooves*. He temporarily abandoned these potboilers upon beginning an affair with Gloria Swanson, the reigning queen of Hollywood silent films. "Gloria needs handling," said a tipster who informed him of her waywardness with money. Swanson, already married three times, was twenty-eight, a good age for a film star to be in those days when cameras and lighting required very young actresses. Joe placed her in the infamous *Queen Kelly*, directed by the daring perfectionist Erich von Stroheim. Kennedy ultimately witheld the film, which portrays a self-giving prostitute nun, from distribution, ostensibly for moral reasons. In the 1950 movie *Sunset Boulevard*, in which Swanson brilliantly played an aging movie actress and von Stroheim played her butler and confidant, a sequence from *Queen Kelly* is shown. Joe managed to hand the actress much of the financial loss for *Queen Kelly* and to offset his own loss through winnings on Swanson's first talking picture, *The Trespasser*. Their romance ended when, according to the actress, she questioned his opinion on a small matter, and Joe chose to return to New York. Recognizing the shakiness of the economy, he sold his common stock holdings just before the stock market crash of 1929.

By the end of the 1920s Joe and Rose Kennedy had eight children. Raising young Kennedys was a joint project. Rose superintended them with both vigor and painstaking care, keeping files on them, strategically planting reminder notes or abbreviated paper lectures, placing clocks in every room so the children would not be late for dinner or Mass. The father, when home, ruled the children firmly. Rose schooled the children in such points as the correct use of "I" and "me" so that they could speak properly in Joe's presence, and before dinner they were required to read news stories tacked on a bulletin board in preparation for discussion with him. Sometimes the family conversation concerned the fundamental national issues of the day. At other times one of the children assumed the role of a Founding Father and argued points based on *The Federalist Papers*. While many of the "conversations" consisted of Joe's lectures or questions eliciting factual responses from his sons, the overall effect created in young Jack Kennedy a craving to read and a capacity to memorize masses of information. In general, the boys attended Protestant preparatory schools, whereas the girls were sent to Catholic schools.

The Kennedy family compound at Hyannis Port was especially fit for the training of male offspring. It was a place for calisthenics at dawn; Wheaties for breakfast; lectures from the father; and practice in the patrician sport of sailing, perfected by the elder Kennedy as he followed the boys in a separate boat, barking out their mistakes over a bullhorn. The sport was patrician; but the concentration was on winning, not on the graceful and courteous excellence of the *aristoi*. "Don't play unless you can be captain," Joe Kennedy is supposed to have proclaimed, along with "Second place is failure." A son who performed badly was sometimes forced to eat in the kitchen, and Joe Kennedy, Jr., once won a race with an oversized sail. Is it that the father, so eager for entrance into the upper classes, was forever simply missing the point, which is that the well-mannered sportsman plays for the sake of good manners? Or was he quite consciously seeking triumphal vindication on his own terms in place of acceptance on theirs, confident that after a correct interval of haughty rejection, older society will yield to new money and power?

Joe Kennedy courted the socially established Anglo-American classes by using tactics that violated the codes to which those classes claimed to subscribe. Those tactics brought wealth to Joe, which he used to buy for his children an education in more polite ways of living. His aggressiveness would become a component in the characters of his offspring. In Jack Kennedy that aggressiveness was combined with an element of fastidious withdrawal which suggests that in him the education took hold.

The local Catholic culture must also have presented mixed messages. The religion of the Nazarene poor has found many formulas for justifying wealth, but at a sacrifice to simple consistency. The local ethnic Catholicism also reconciled piety with hard-bitten ambition and the rough ways of city politics. It further mingled economic progressivism with ideological conservatism. Many layers of social and moral history were compressed in the consciousness of three generations of Kennedys.

Joe's fatherly attention was returned with love and obedience. What children would not admire a father who could introduce them to the cowboy movie star Tom Mix or the sports heros Babe Ruth or Red Grange, and who instantly responded to their letters when away from home? Despite Joe's many trips away, the children correctly sensed that they were always on his mind. Some successful fathers can transmit only their wealth to their children; Joe Kennedy also passed on his unyielding determination. The exception was Rosemary, retarded and, after an operation, cared for at a convent. Joe showed his love for her by making heavy contributions to research on retardation.

Joe Kennedy made another fortune in the stock market by selling short during its plunge from May 1930 to March 1933. Meanwhile, he was interesting himself in politics, particularly in an aspiring presidential candidate, whose steel he had tested during World War I. In 1930 he visited Franklin D. Roosevelt, then governor of New York. The Great Depression had frightened Kennedy, as it had many other American capitalists in the 1930s. Hungry people, he said, could turn "ugly and menacing," and something should be done for them. Roosevelt, of course, did not yet have the credentials that his New Deal would later give him. But Joe Kennedy shrewdly saw in him at least a possibility for national economic initiatives. He raised $150,000 for FDR and traveled with him on several campaign tours; he would always claim to have persuaded William Randolph Hearst to break the convention deadlock that had held FDR back from an early win. The additional $50,000 that he lent the Roosevelt campaign was never repaid, but in company with FDR's son James, Joe went to Europe on a successful postelection trip to import "medicinal" liquor—Ron Rico rum, Haig & Haig Scotch, and Gordon's gin—just in time for the repeal of prohibition.

The important early backer earned a larger reward, somewhat grudging and belated because of opposition from Roosevelt's adviser Louis Howe. A Columbus, Ohio, campaign speech that Kennedy had written for Roosevelt carried a blueprint for the future Securities and Exchange Commission. In 1934 Roosevelt appointed the stock market insider as chairman of the commission, saying, as one practical man might say of another man equally unburdened with scruples, "It takes a thief to catch a thief." Perhaps Joe Kennedy's most effective innovation was to prohibit short sales at a price lower than the last to appear on the stock market ticker. He preferred conscientious self-regulation to new laws but enforced rules strictly against flagrant abusers. Corporate underwriting quadrupled under his management, and Kennedy received considerable praise for his work.

Joe Kennedy left the post in 1935 to write a campaign book, *I'm for Roosevelt,* published the following year, which argued that businessmen should be grateful to FDR for saving capitalism. Actually his journalist friend Arthur Krock did the writing; Kennedy had offered him $5,000 for the job. "It was useful," Joe observed elsewhere, "to have a Roosevelt who had the confidence of the masses," and could mollify them short of more radical programs. But the book embraced government planning uncritically, crediting Roosevelt with every economic gain since 1933. The volume contained at least one line of nonsense: "I have," Joe wrote, "no political ambitions for myself or for my children."

Joe returned to government for a year as head of the Maritime Commission, with the object of invigorating the sickly shipbuilding industry. The great moment followed: his selection in 1938 as ambassador to Great Britain. With this appointment Kennedy had captured a high citadel of the Anglo-

American aristocracy. Not yet believing that events in Europe deserved his concentrated attention, Roosevelt had evidently thought it a "grand joke" to tweak the lion's mane by appointing an unreconstructed Irishman to the Court of Saint James. When he first heard the suggestion, FDR "laughed so hard he almost fell out of his wheelchair."

The hot-tempered, gum-chewing ambassador delivered Roosevelt a pile of trouble. He called the queen of England a "cute trick" (he later revised that to a "dowdy housewife") and Churchill a "heavy drinker," but those references paled beside his apparent remark to the German ambassador, "I'm for Hitler." Family, not country, motivated Joe. In one speech at Aberdeen, he wrote: "I should like to ask you all if you know of any dispute or controversy existing in the world which is worth the life of your son, or of anyone else's son?" He also feared that communism would emerge from the rubble of a war. His appointment was proving disastrous for the United States. He praised the Munich settlement, saying he could not imagine going to war for Czechoslovakia. In 1938 after Munich he told the Navy League: "The democracies and dictators should cooperate for the common good." FDR, unprepared for amicable remarks about the Fascists, informed Kennedy that he did not want his ambassador to continue arguing against American intervention in the European war that began in September 1939. Kennedy returned home in 1940. Because of an indiscreet interview, in which Joe told reporters that "democracy is finished in England," he exhausted his credit with Roosevelt and learned a painful lesson about discretion in politics. That episode put an end to his public career, but not the use of his influence on behalf of his sons, who were now to take up his march upon the fortresses of the Brahmin class.

The father's ambitions for his offspring fixed first on his oldest son, Joe, Jr., who resembled the elder Kennedy in aggressiveness and drive. Perhaps the son's pronouncement "Someday I'll be president" bespoke a sense that his father's legacy and obligation lay in his ruggedly schooled body and mind. He took lessons in elocution, a politically serviceable art that could refine the Kennedy combativeness with the polish of an upper-class education. Joe, Jr., like his father, was sometimes not particularly agreeable and sometimes immensely charming. Edward Kennedy recalls that his brother once dared him into successively more dangerous dives off Eden Roc—at Hotel du Câp D'Antibes on the French Riviera—into the Mediterranean until his father intervened. Joe was the kind of boy, a classmate at Choate Academy recalled, who "couldn't pass a hat without squashing it or leave an unprotected shin unkicked." Jack Kennedy, whom the young Joe bullied unmercifully, would later set aside the conventional pieties toward the dead and speak of Joe's "hot temper" and his "sardonic half smile as though he were kidding you." An early photograph shows the two brothers holding hands, with little Jack grimacing because Joe was squeezing his hand so hard. Still, when his father was absent, Joe dutifully helped to bring up his younger brothers and sisters, who loved as well as feared him. Joe's Catholicism was rigorous, and he prayed nightly at his bedside. His senior thesis at Harvard, "Intervention in Spain," favored the Fascist dictator Francisco Franco, and a visit to Spain in 1938 confirmed his view. Joe approved of the Munich settlement and in that year wrote to a friend that the Germans were a "marvelous people," whom it would be "tough . . . to keep . . . from getting what they want." He related to his father his impression of the Jews in Germany: "Their methods had been quite unscrupulous. This dislike of the Jews . . . [is] . . . well-founded." In truth, Joe, Jr., could as well have been referring to his own father's clannishness, uncouth manners, and financial unscrupulousness.

The aggressive Joe, Jr., was a major presence in the early life of Jack Kennedy. Jack needed twenty-eight stitches after he and his brother Joe collided on their Brookline block, playing at a game that involved running at each other. Joe's "pugnacious personality," Jack was to remember, "smoothed out but it was a problem in my boyhood." At Choate, Jack wrote his father about a hazing given his brother for roughhousing: "All the sixth formers had a swat or two. Did the sixth formers kick him. O Man he was all blisters, they almost paddled the life out of him. What I wouldn't have given to be a sixth former." While Jack easily made friends in preparatory school, Joe had difficulty in doing so, though he made a favorable impression on the headmaster. By the time of their Harvard years, Jack was beginning to outdo his older brother in both scholarship and popularity.

After college Joe joined the Navy. Holding the leadership of his Florida naval base's Holy Name Society became a vehicle for asserting his vigorous Catholicism: he would douse his comrades with cold water, not sparing his mates of other religions, to awaken them for early Mass. Joe's competitiveness with Jack persisted during this time. After Jack had won glory in the South Pacific as a PT boat commander, Joe brooded, "clenching and unclenching his fists," after toasts to the young hero. He did not even call his father from Florida to tell him about Jack's dangerous undertaking.

Later, from his naval air force base in Great Britain, Joe unnecessarily risked the lives of his crew by flying too close to a German-held island off the French coast. Despite his father's worried warning not to "force your luck," Joe seized a bizarre opportunity. The military had conceived a plan to send a gigantic bomb on an aircraft drone against the German V-1 rocket sites in France; volunteer airmen were to set the fuse on the bomb before they parachuted to safety while still over British soil. Six such army missions had already failed with one fatality. Joe volunteered to lead the first naval attempt. On a bleak summer day just after the Normandy invasion, a PB4Y loaded with eleven tons of explosives took off with young Kennedy at the controls, despite a warning to him about a dangerous flaw in the firing system. The plane blew up over southern England; it was the largest airborne explosion over the country during the war. Joe's upbringing had glorified achievement and risk-taking; it was the same up-bringing that would produce a president of the United States. Joe had left a message for his father: "If I don't come back, tell my dad . . . that I love him very much." Months afterward it was discovered that Joe's intended target had been abandoned before the attack. In 1948, Jack lost his sister, the vivacious Kathleen ("Kick"), in another plane crash; and Kathleen's English officer husband had died in the war in the same year as Joe.

Brighter and more bookish than Joe, Jack Kennedy was making his own way in the world. As a boy Jack told his mother, "If you study too much you're liable to go crazy" and inquired which was his father's sweet tooth. Once when Jack's mother was at church on Good Friday, she urged all the children to wish for a happy death; the others acquiesced, but Jack said he would prefer to wish for two puppies. He was the only child who could get away with being late for a meal or leaving his room in disarray. Perhaps this immunity from punishment came about because he was ill so often; he almost died of scarlet fever in 1920. He read omnivorously in bed recuperating from one disease or another. He won popularity, although not high grades, at Choate preparatory school and became the school prankster, once abetting a plan to stuff all the pillows from a dormitory into a friend's room. An acquaintance was to remember an English teacher's telling Jack that he had a facility for writing and recalls that Jack shouted out answers at the radio during the quiz show "Information Please." A history teacher said Jack had one "of the few great minds" he had encountered. And Jack was the only student at Choate to read *The New York Times* every day. He was evidently following the road of self-improvement laid out by his father. At Harvard Jack's academic life was marred by a poor freshman year but improved steadily, finally to a B + average and the dean's list. The political scientist Arthur Holcombe gave him B's, later commenting: "He had no interest in causes, his approach was that of a young scientist in a laboratory." Bruce Hopper called him "surprisingly able, when he gets down to work" and spoke of the "felicity of phrase and graceful presentation" in Jack's senior thesis, which earned him a magna cum laude.

The thesis, which was published in 1940 as *Why England Slept*, argues that democracies in the absence of immediate emergency encourage private aims, which at the time of fascism's rise hindered rearmament. The book praises Churchill for evoking British national purpose, much as Jack would call for a national renewal in his 1960 presidential campaign. *Why England Slept* argues not for intervention but for rearmament. Jack wrote the manuscript in chapter-by-chapter drafts for his thesis adviser Hopper. But before publication, his father ensured it was rewritten professionally. Jack Kennedy's own early intellectual curiosity is nevertheless as indisputable as his charm. Coming up with the topic in the first place reflected his interest in current events and politics. "Very argumentative in a nice way," an acquaintance styled him at this time. Ambassador to Moscow Charles Bohlen found him "an extremely personable, attractive, and bright young man." One of his many girl friends complained that "he listened to *every* radio news broadcast."

As he grew to manhood Kennedy's character also responded to a series of unusual illnesses and pain caused in part by a reckless devotion to sports. At Choate Jack had more absences for illness than any other boy in his class. He initially entered not Harvard where he would be near his brother Joe but Princeton where he withdrew to a hospital for treatment of hepatitis, asthma, and a back weakened since childhood. At Harvard, though he weighed a scant 150 pounds, he insisted on playing football and hung out with athletes. Once he remained on the field even after cracking a leg bone colliding with an equipment wagon; and one day in scrimmage he ruptured a spinal disc. During summers Jack toured Europe, making a commitment to General Franco's Spain that was noticeably weaker than Joe, Jr.'s. Jack told his father that the nonfascist government under attack by Franco and his mercenaries was "in the right morally speaking as its program was similar to the New Deal." In London he was able to spend a semester doing much of his thesis research firsthand, using connections provided him by his ambassador father. Before leaving for home Jack came down with jaundice.

After graduation from Harvard Jack entered Stanford University to study economics and business and beautiful young women. Following ten weeks in California and a tour of Latin America he decided to enlist. Both the army and the navy rejected him because of his weak back. But a political push from his father gained him the rank of ensign and a job in the Office of Naval Intelligence in Washington. A brief affair ensued between Jack and Inga Arvad, a beautiful journalist who, allegedly a Miss Denmark, had caught the eye of der Führer at the Berlin Olympic Games of 1936. He granted a private interview to the blue-eyed blonde, whom he labeled a "perfect example of Nordic beauty." Hermann Göring gave her an award for winning a beauty contest. All this interested the indefatigable J. Edgar Hoover, head of the Federal Bureau of Investigation, who recorded intimate conversations between Jack and Inga. Jack was transferred to seamanship school at Northwestern University and then to the South Pacific to command a PT boat. During all this time his back pained him fiercely; while in training school he slept on a table instead of a bed.

On these light, highly maneuverable craft Jack might relive his Nantucket sailing experience. They suggested the grace and élan of sailing, and it was that quality rather than any special military effectiveness that characterized them. The young commander of PT-109 once raced his boat homeward toward the dock, cutting the motors at the last moment, and ramming the structure. One dark, misty night he was on an important patrol, with engines improperly set and no one on watch, when a Japanese destroyer striking with tremendous force neatly sliced his PT in two, setting it afire and spilling the crew into the waters near the Solomon Islands. That night, August 1, 1943, two men died, but Jack towed a badly burned mate across a strong current at sea back to one-half of his boat and then for four hours across miles of open sea to Plum Pudding Island. During the next days his shrewd efforts to save his crew won him front page headlines in American newspapers. His courage was a counterpart to the endurance of illness that plagued so many of his days. Returned stateside for an operation on his back after some further misadventures at sea, he suffered still more excruciating pain in the area of a gaping hole left by the surgeon.

During his slow recuperation in Arizona, Jack and his father spent a long time each day talking on the phone, conversations that brought the two closer. Jack replaced Joe, Jr., in his father's political plans. "I told him Joe was dead," reads a later comment by the elder Kennedy, "and that it was his responsibility." Joseph Kennedy wanted his oldest son to be in politics, though "wanted," according to Jack, "isn't the right word. He demanded it. You know my father." Jack was unsure whether politics was the right career for him, but his father had enough confidence and enthusiasm for the two of them. In 1946 Jack ran for Congress from a Democratic district in Cambridge, Massachusetts.

Joe Kennedy was turning his attention to midtown New York City real estate and to the Chicago Merchandise Mart; both projects advanced his fortune by giant strides. Joe raised rents and evicted tenants with abandon. An adviser was John Reynolds, who had made tens of millions for Cardinal Francis Spellman's Archdiocese of New York. Joe's fortune has been estimated to be about $200 million or more by 1960.

I I

The Rise to Stardom, 1945–1960

TRUE TO HIS LINEAGE Jack Kennedy developed into a good politician. From 1945 to 1960 he followed a twisting, uncertain course in foreign and domestic affairs that reflected the changing moods of the country. Jack's immediate postwar career was expressive of the conformist Cold War anxieties of the late 1940s. But later in the 1950s he moved restlessly, along with many other restless Americans, to a destination he never clearly articulated. By the end of his life, his presidency would incorporate much of what was to become the liberalism of the 1960s, which his brothers Robert and Edward were consciously to carry farther.

The current circumstances and experiences of the Kennedy family contrasted with the conservatism of the elder Joseph Kennedy. The Kennedys remained outsiders, never full members of an upper class that was resistant to change. At the same time, they were not self-made and therefore were not tempted either to assume that everyone can make it without government aid or to pull down the ladder of opportunity because of fear that others would displace them. The family's roots were planted deeply in traditions of urban Irish Democratic politics. The local urban Democratic party, in spite of the narrowness and corruption sometimes associated with it, had its own agenda of social reform; it was part of a national party that Franklin Roosevelt's New Deal had set upon a reformist course. Moreover, the family's own fortunes and character had been created out of action and had no identification except with action as a program in itself. The elder Joe Kennedy had never given himself wholly to the sometimes predatory economics of conservatism. He often subordinated the privacy of his ruthless business career to his hunger for popular acceptance and public service. Jack Kennedy and his brothers, then, were susceptible to the influence of current events.

Joe Kennedy, who rarely left things to chance if he could do otherwise, had prepared the way for his son Jack's first congressional campaign in 1946. The year before, at the request of the governor, Joe had cochaired a commission to study the economic needs of Massachusetts. It is likely that he sold his Haig & Haig Scotch franchise to improve public appearances. After World War II Joe arranged for Jack to get the very respectable job of a newspaper reporter for the Hearst chain, which touted him as "the PT hero who would explain the GI viewpoint." The young war hero covered the founding of the United Nations in San Francisco, the Potsdam Conference, and the postwar elections in Britain, where he made the shrewd observation that Churchill might lose. His editor thought that his story of a possible British Labour victory was absurd and rewrote it to predict a Conservative triumph. Jack's prediction, however, came true.

Jack ran for the congressional seat in the area of Cambridge, Massachusetts, the same area that Boston's former mayor James Michael Curley had held. (Soon a judge would send the popular mayor to Danbury prison for violating numerous federal laws.) Curley had suggested that Jack, since he bore both the names Fitzgerald and Kennedy, might forgo campaigning and enjoy the Florida sun until Congress convened. The elder Kennedy had other ideas. The son must plunge into the Democratic primary and learn about working-class families and city wards with their respected leaders and rites of patronage. The young Harvard-educated Jack, though handicapped by his bad back and the lingering effects of a wartime bout with malaria, was forced to learn what his ancestors had come to know through political osmosis.

Jack delivered his early campaign speeches too swiftly, and he lacked political presence. Also, his figure was gaunt. But terming himself a "fighting conservative" (a phrase that he associated with Churchill) in a period when returning veterans were enormously popular, he gently reminded the voters of his own war hero's record. His father promulgated the same message not so subtly by arranging to have placed on every empty bus or subway seat the *Reader's Digest's* condensed version of the PT-109 story. Jack's father was a great help: for a weak speech the son first received praise from the elder Kennedy; then, no longer defensive, the candidate was told his faults, which Joe had carefully compiled from listeners in the audience. Jack's public speaking improved. His interests lay mainly in international politics, and the congressional race was but a means to playing a future role on that stage.

Both friends and family pitched in to help in the 1946 congressional campaign. Even fourteen-year-old Teddy ran errands. An advertising agency hired by Joe Kennedy oversaw the roles of amateurs like Jack's Navy friend Red Fay, as well as of the Kennedy family members, including old Honey Fitz. The determined patriarch Joe also artfully donated large sums to popular Catholic charities and helped establish the Joseph P. Kennedy, Jr., Chapter of the Veterans of Foreign Wars. To undercut the vote of a well-known city councilman, Joseph Russo, Joe ran a second candidate of that name in the Democratic primary campaign. And Joe gave other primary candidates thousands of dollars to enter or leave the race as expediency dictated. Jack, at twenty-nine, won the primary handily, assuring election to Congress in the heavily Democratic district.

The candidate was by nature reserved, skeptical, and averse to schmaltz; his reticence in campaigning was a departure from backslapping, gladhanding Boston politics. He rarely attended wakes, for instance, unless he had known the deceased. Yet his personal manner was exceptionally casual; in the congressional dining room he often appeared in a sweater and sneakers. A young man of distinction had arrived in Washington. But what were the beliefs that inhabited his very private mind?

Jack's first letter to constituents complained about bad acoustics in the House chamber, poor lighting, and rudeness of members who talked or read newspapers while others spoke. Yet some of his comments during the period reflected the intellectual curiosity that certain of his teachers had observed. He startled the economist Barbara Ward on several occasions with his unpredictable, open-minded queries about the political process, the welfare state, and socialized medicine. She noted his "extraordinary intellectual vividness," which sufficiently described Jack's virtues in those days. The one job that sparked his interest was membership on the Labor and Education Committee, where he demonstrated skills in interrogating witnesses. His presentation was factual and direct. He also demonstrated his startling independence during the congressional years by refusing, alone among the Massachusetts delegation, to request a pardon for James Michael Curley. Jack Kennedy, he seemed to be saying, was no Irish political hack. And when on the floor of the House, in response to American Legion opposition to a housing bill, he remarked that the leaders of the Legion had not had "a constructive thought for the benefit of the country since 1918," he won much support. The political benefits of the gesture did not undermine its freshness and independence. Jack was the only Boston area congressman to vote in favor of the St. Lawrence Seaway, which Bay State residents feared would raid their Massachusetts commerce.

On foreign policy, except for some uncertainties expressed briefly in the utopian mood of 1945, Jack Kennedy followed his father, his church, and the times. Communism was a monolithic worldwide menace. Franklin D. Roosevelt had given eastern Europe to the Reds at Yalta. The White House and the Department of State had "lost China." At an informal Harvard seminar in 1950, John Kennedy declared his liking for Senator Joseph R. McCarthy and his pleasure at the young Richard Nixon's victory over the liberal California Senator Helen Gahagan Douglas, and he announced his desire to get "the foreigners off our backs." On the House floor he talked of "Hottentots." Liberals then distrusted the young congressman who, it seemed to them, was the image of his outspoken father.

Jack differed from his father in his increasing internationalism of the Democratic Cold War variety. He voted for a stronger air force in 1948 instead of tax cuts, something his father would not have done. In fact, Jack favored the Truman Doctrine, virtually the entire Marshall Plan and European Recovery Program, and, though he expressed some reservations about the Korean War, almost all of the Democratic administration's foreign policy initiatives in Europe and Asia. Jack's father had a conservative's distrust of free-spending liberal Wilsonian internationalism. Joe looked on Truman's interventions in western Europe as an example of a liberal's compulsion to waste American resources. "What business is it of ours," the elder Kennedy asked a University of Virginia audience, "to support French colonial policy in Indo-China or to achieve Mr. Syngman Rhee's concepts of democracy in Korea?" Leave communism alone and it would breed internal dissension: Joe correctly predicted the split between Communist China and the Soviet Union. Gradually he made fewer foreign policy pronouncements, fearing they would taint his son's ambitions. The division between Kennedy generations was an instance of the split between prewar isolationists and postwar cold warriors.

On domestic issues Jack voted all over the spectrum. He derided liberal "do-gooders" and voted against funds for hospital construction, federal support for rural cooperatives, aid to the Navajo and Hopi Indians, money for public libraries in areas without any, and a bill prohibiting employment discrimination. But he voted in favor of extending social security benefits, a minimum wage law, and compromise legislation on medical care for the poor. His major interest was in better housing, particularly for returning veterans, and he voted for almost any bill that would help his constituents. On the Labor and Education Committee he took a middle course, opposing the antilabor Taft-Hartley bill yet expressing dislike for labor leaders, many of whom he viewed as corrupt racketeers. His ideology, like the country's, was blurred, except on the issue of domestic communism.

On the Labor and Education Committee, Kennedy contributed to that issue when he exposed the Communist Harold Christoffel of the United Auto Workers for committing perjury. Kennedy was angry, with perhaps a veteran's anger, that Christoffel's union had interfered with the rearmament effort in 1941 by conducting a strike. Kennedy's shrewd and persistent attack was an opening salvo in the House war against the Communist party. At Harvard in 1952, when a speaker had linked Alger Hiss with Joseph McCarthy, to the disfavor of each, Jack responded by saying "How dare you couple the name of a great American patriot with that of a traitor?" In 1954 with such unlikely cosponsors as Hubert Humphrey and Wayne Morse, he worked for the Communist Control Act, which put the Democrats safely on the side of antilibertarian red-baiting.

The House of Representatives seemed to bore him, perhaps because illness stalked him. Addison's disease struck him hard in the late 1940s. The resulting adrenal insufficiency that made him susceptible to secondary infections might have killed him had not oral cortisone come into use at that time. He was very anemic, suffered from acute allergies, and had a hole in his back, which was left from an earlier operation, that kept getting reinfected. Two drastic spinal operations, in late 1954 and early 1955, pulled him back from death. His fatalism and an attendant self-confidence may have been products of his lifelong struggle against illness. And that struggle, far more than the glamorous exterior and the rhetoric of strife and confrontation, measured the strength of the man. But struggle and strength of that kind had no public, collective enactment. Much of the Kennedy vocabulary of the later years, the exhortations to national effort and determination, spoke of a shadow world of half-defined combatants, shades cast by a real war, private and interior.

As his House attendance dwindled, Jack's one-night stands with beautiful women multiplied. This promiscuity, which may have been intensified by his cortisone shots, had a possible basis in a British doctor's prediction that he would probably die before reaching forty. One woman he dated in those years remembered him as a man driven, rushed, grabbing at her along with anything else he wanted. This behavior also resembled the well-known philandering of Jack's father and older brother.

Jack Kennedy was looking toward the United States Senate; on trips home he frequently spoke to various Massachusetts audiences and avoided his safe congressional district almost entirely. He often spent four days campaigning, returning to Washington for votes on Tuesday through Thursdays. The Kennedy target bore the name of an old enemy family: Senator Henry Cabot Lodge, Jr., up for reelection in 1952. It would be a much different campaign from those in his safe Catholic district, but a strong showing among Catholic voters would still be essential. The election also provided Jack with an opportunity to outdo his competitive father and achieve his own national identity.

Kennedy money flooded Massachusetts as the 1952 election approached. "We're going to sell Jack like soap flakes," his father announced. Once again large gifts in the Kennedy name went to charities, notably the Italian-American Charitable Society. "Dad" wrote to Jack in 1952 of another group: "We might send them a check for $1,000 only because it is this year." Jack wrote plainly enough to a California acquaintance that as the 1952 campaign approached, his father's charitable foundation "has been concentrating its donations . . . in the Massachusetts areas." Discovering no limit on the number of committees to which $1,000 could be contributed, Joe created a series of "improvement" groups aimed at fishing, shoemaking, and textiles. And most notably, Joe lent a half million dollars to the McCarthyite publisher of the Boston *Post*. "You know we had to buy that f. . . paper, or I'd have been licked," Jack would tell a Harvard classmate. The ethics that had served well in 1946 served again. On one occasion both Lodge and Kennedy were to receive awards from an Italian-American group. The man who was bringing Lodge's decoration somehow disappeared from a train with the result that Jack would get his award—and the resulting publicity—first. Lodge was under the additional disadvantage of having alienated supporters of Robert Taft because Lodge had been instrumental in persuading General Dwight D. Eisenhower to run in the 1952 Republican presidential primaries.

The careful organization of the senatorial campaign derived largely from the able assistance of Robert Kennedy, with whom Jack had become particularly close during a world trip in 1951 and whose hard-driving tactics soon became legendary. Serving as campaign manager, Robert first decided to gather a list of names nominating Jack that would exceed the minuscule requirement by a quarter million. Each signatory was sent a letter of thanks prior to the election. Then the famous Kennedy tea parties came into their widest use. All of the siblings hosted these parties, but Rose, as in 1946, proved the most adept in the family. She wore a simple dress when appearing before a group of lower-middle-class housewives, and then in her darkened limousine she changed to a bejeweled gown to speak a few words at an upper-class charity function. Jack attacked Lodge, a capable internationalist senator, for spending too little time on domestic issues. In a little-noticed debate, Kennedy aggressively outdid Lodge in discussing international issues. To a Jewish audience, Jack pointed out that *he* was running for office, not his father. This time the PT-109 article went out to every home in Massachusetts.

Kennedy campaign workers tried to phone each voter at least twice. Archbishop Richard Cushing of Boston contributed to the swell in the closing days of the campaign by baptizing Robert and Ethel's baby just before election day, keeping the Kennedy name in a favorable light before the many Irish and Italian voters. Jack won the tight race by about 70,000 votes, while the Republican presidential candidate Eisenhower swept Massachusetts.

After defeating Lodge, Kennedy claimed that it was his years of hard work and not the Kennedy name and wealth which had made the difference. He had worked, of course; the Kennedys worked at anything that suited their ambitions. But if John was revealing any sensitivity over the power that his family's wealth gave him, he need not have worried about adverse public reaction. The Kennedys, a campaign manager has pointed out, can spend any amount of money on political contests because the public knows that they have the money. Americans, who pride themselves on a work ethic, are little troubled when there is a demonstrable absence of any correlation between work and wealth.

The next year Jack, one of Washington's most eligible bachelors, married "up" to Jacqueline Bouvier, daughter of financier John Bouvier and the very *Social Register* Mrs. Hugh D. Auchincloss, of Newport and New York. The ancestry, grace, and beauty of the bride conformed to what the Kennedys were trying to cultivate. An alumna of Miss Porter's School, Vassar College, and the Sorbonne, Jackie translated several articles in French for Jack, including some on Vietnam. During their courtship Jack gave her books on American history and his prized John Buchan's *Pilgrim's Way,* a tale of elite heroism in colonial Britain. It surely intrigued Jackie that Jack talked of running for president. She had worked as a journalist for some years and later in her life would work as a book editor. She relished flippancy: when the family discussed where the 1960 presidential convention should be held, she suggested Acapulco. The marriage was not partic-

ularly happy. Jack sometimes went on vacations with his bud-
dies, and he had many affairs with beautiful women well into
his White House years. He was not on hand when Jackie suffered the first of two miscarriages before eventually giving
birth to two handsome children, Caroline and John, Jr. A
spender of fabled sums, Jacqueline allegedly accepted a million dollars from Joe Kennedy to remain married during his
son's presidency. Jackie's attractiveness and social finish, as
well as the couple's appealing children, lent themselves to the
later public perception of the Kennedy style. On a 1961 trip
to Europe Jack introduced himself as "the man who accompanied Jacqueline Kennedy to Paris"; wearing a demure pill-
box hat, she looked more like a Hollywood star than did many
reigning movie queens.

The office of senator provided fresh evidence that Jack was
aiming at the presidency. He worked now as if he were a senator from New England, not just Massachusetts. And his
heated denunciations of communism, increasingly unfashion-
able, almost ceased. Privately he hinted that Senator Joe
McCarthy had gone too far in his personal war against communism. Also, on the television news program "Meet the
Press," Jack said that the government had gotten rid of most
of its subversives, a belief that did not comport with the ideological craving of the red-hunters to have an eternal enemy.
Having learned of what he called the "fires of nationalism,"
he was apparently capable of seeing more significance in third
world struggles than in a war between communism and the
West. British and French colonialism he regarded as outmoded and dangerous. He condemned the French for their
activities in Vietnam and told an audience in 1952 that the
United States should not send troops there. Yet Jack was the
only senator to miss recording his vote to censure his family's
friend Joe McCarthy, on whose investigatory staff Robert
Kennedy had been employed. Even though hospitalized for a
painful back operation, Jack could have paired with another
senator against McCarthy. Instead, he took the safe course of

opposing the tactics of McCarthy's lieutenants and asserting that McCarthy had done no damage to United States foreign policy.

It is hard even to guess what went on in Jack Kennedy's mind regarding the McCarthy issue. Was he being stubbornly loyal to his family and to his Irish Catholic constituents who certainly embraced the anticommunism of the times? Or, like Lyndon Johnson, was he a political bellwether in the 1950s, striving to break away from an embarrassing past without offending his flock? Whatever the answer, his moral position was weak. Eleanor Roosevelt wrote accurately in her memoirs: "A public servant must clearly indicate that he understands the harm that McCarthyism did to our country and that he opposes it actively, so that one would feel sure that he would always do so in the future."

Senator Kennedy gained a national reputation in 1956 with the publication of *Profiles in Courage,* which won a Pulitzer Prize in 1957. It is a readable book of essays on American public figures who displayed political courage. Kennedy did not exactly write it, hardly wrote it at all, in fact. He wrote some rough drafts of a couple of chapters, but it was composed mainly by his newly acquired liberal adviser and publicist Ted Sorensen, who has remarked, "I prepared the materials on which the book is based." In recent years the production of a ghostwritten book is a conventional episode in the packaging of a politician as a statesman-commentator. But Kennedy managed to win a Pulitzer Prize for a book he had not written. The most charming account of how he got the prize is that the trustees of Columbia University, in their wisdom, thought it a wonderful book for boys who might aspire to be statesmen, and thus casually overruled the academic advisory committee's choices. A more sinister account is that Joe Kennedy's friend Arthur Krock influenced the trustees on behalf of Joe's son.

The typical act of political courage, of course, is to defy on principle the wishes of a constituency. A book about that kind of courage is not an actual instance of it. Voters will not take offense at a politician's telling of the virtues of independence; it is only the exercise of that independence which will test their tolerance. On the issue of Curley's pardon and the Seaway, Kennedy did go against the apparent feelings of his electorate. It is more significant that the book depicts courage as interior, a self-control under stress. That is the kind of courage which Kennedy must have developed to endure the long illnesses to which he never psychologically succumbed. It is a tighter and steadier courage than are the discharges of resolute energy that Kennedy's speeches were to urge upon the nation as he approached 1960. But perhaps it is not far different from the temperament that Kennedy's presidential foreign policies demanded, while right-wingers wanted something more emotionally gratifying than the measured response to the Communist sealing of East Berlin or the complex relationships with Moscow that progressed from the blockade of Cuba to the test ban treaty.

Another clue about Kennedy is his depiction of the reconstruction era as "a black nightmare the South never could forget." That quotation reflects the historical view of the post–Civil War South still widely held in the 1950s. The civil rights movement was only just beginning, and most American historians had not yet fully discovered the racist premises on which the old interpretations of Reconstruction had rested. Senator Kennedy's record on civil rights reflects little curiosity about the issue. He would court segregationists in his campaign for president. On four central civil rights votes in the Senate during the 1950s, he sided twice with liberals and, on issues of greater importance, twice with the South. He voted to require jury trials for accused violators of the 1957 Civil Rights Act, at a time when few Southern white jurors respected the legal rights of black people. Vice President Richard Nixon, a figure just barely within the liberal wing of the ideologically divided Republican party, denounced the Senate's adoption of the jury trial amendment as "a vote against the right to vote."

Was Kennedy's record a reflection of indifference? His earlier performance on the House Committee on the District of Columbia had included opposition to a sales tax that would have unfairly affected poor blacks, and he had energetically supported home rule, which conservatives opposed because much of the District's population was black. In 1952 he unsuccessfully argued that the Senate should pass a rule against filibusters, which Southerners had used to block civil rights bills. He wanted to make cloture possible with a mere majority vote. The next year he picked Ted Sorensen of Nebraska as his chief adviser. He liked Sorensen for preferring practical liberals to emotional liberals. But Sorensen had a pronounced and impressively early record of civil rights activity, including the founding of a chapter of the Congress of Racial Equality in his home state. Sorensen was also a conscientious objector during World War II, which made his selection a testimony to Kennedy's open-mindedness. His conservative votes on civil rights, then, do not suggest moral indifference. Instead, they mean that the issue was not central to him, that he was not yet the champion of the committed liberalism that was to gain so much from the unforeseen fortunes of his presidency.

Whatever the reasons for his contradictory voting record on civil rights, Kennedy as a potential candidate for the presidency needed to acquire a larger following than only Roman Catholics and urban northeasterners. In the election of 1928 Herbert Hoover broke the Solid South, winning all but four Southern states against the Roman Catholic governor of New York, Alfred E. Smith. The postwar era brought some resurgence of anti-Catholicism, which gained from Francis Cardinal Spellman's attack on Eleanor Roosevelt for writing a newspaper column that did little more than praise separation of church and state. The reactionary Spellman also prevailed on New York politicians to ban *The Nation* from the city's public schools—it had already been banned in the libraries of most Catholic institutions—because of a series of articles condemning the church's hierarchical power. In 1950 Kennedy himself had stumbled by supporting federal aid to Catholic parochial schools with an intensity that was not healthy for a national politician. Fortunately for Kennedy, the Supreme Court later rendered such aid respectable by delivering a five to four decision favoring it. Other skilled national Democrats, most notably Franklin Roosevelt and Harry Truman, were able to bridge with comparative ease the gap between the liberal North and the largely conservative South. But they were Protestants.

Kennedy was reaching to the South and to non-Catholics. He cultivated conservative Southerners as personal friends, notably Congressman John Rankin of Mississippi and Senators Richard Russell, Spessard Holland, and George Smathers. Even when advancing New England economic programs, he tried not to alienate economically competing states in the South. At the same time, his strategy aimed toward putting his Catholicism to use. Before his party's 1956 convention Sorensen leaked the Bailey memorandum, named after a Connecticut Democratic leader, arguing that a Catholic candidate would strengthen a national ticket. The significance of Al Smith, the memorandum argued, was the inroads he had made with urban Catholic men and women, not his defeat in 1928, a time of immense prosperity that automatically ensured the victory of his Republican opponent. The big difference between 1928 and 1956 was a substantial increase in the Catholic population and its greater concentration in states with large electoral votes. A dangerous sign in that constituency, the memo argued, was President Eisenhower's strong showing among Catholic voters in 1952.

The publication of *Profiles in Courage* drew the attention of Hollywood's Dore Schary, who had produced a color film history of the Democratic party for the Democratic National Committee. What better narrator than the author of a best-seller on political integrity, whose effective television presence had become increasingly noticeable? Kennedy did a superb job of tracing the party's origins from Jefferson and Jackson to its encounter with postwar communism. He then added to his luster with a stirring presidential nominating speech for Adlai Stevenson. *The New York Times,* pronouncing Kennedy a "movie star," was offering an important insight into his sensational rise to prominence.

In throwing open the nomination for vice president, Stevenson did little to ease the minds of those who thought him indecisive. Kennedy went for it. In a thrilling race against Senator Estes Kefauver of Tennessee, he fell behind at the last moment and lost. Yet the "churning up," as he termed it, had made him an attractive national figure. He might have won the nomination had he not voted for a Republican program of flexible agricultural price supports unpopular with farmers, a genuine vote of political courage. The narrowness of Kennedy's loss demonstrated his strength, and the loss itself saved him from identification with a losing presidential bid. The speeches he had made during the campaign, some 150 of them, solidified his own reputation and broadened his political contacts.

Senator Kennedy returned to Washington in 1957 as a member of the Senate Select Committee on Improper Activities in the Labor or Management Field, the famous McClellan Committee. The committee introduced Jack to liberal labor leaders such as Walter Reuther. But it gave him—and his brother Bob, who would later stalk his quarry relentlessly—well-publicized opportunities to pursue such rogues as Jimmy Hoffa and Dave Beck, both of the Teamsters' Union. Kennedy wrote legislation to reform corrupt labor practices and at the same time to soften provisions of the Taft-Hartley Act; though the bill passed the Senate with only one dissent, it died in the House. To Kennedy's detriment, other legislation that was far less favorable to labor eventually came out of the McClellan Committee and survived into law.

Kennedy gained further attention when, in a two-part speech on the Senate floor, he used his important position on the Foreign Relations Committee to denounce France for refusing to grant independence to Algeria. He urged that the

United States bring pressure toward that end. President Eisenhower dismissed the matter as an internal French problem. But liberals loved Kennedy's talk. It was with them that he now had to consolidate his position, because they had long been suspicious of him and his family.

Most of the liberal legislative proposals of the twentieth century have been enacted into law: time always seems to be, if not on the side of liberal politicians or of some encompassing spirit of liberalism, at least on the side of the specific policies the liberals have espoused. The late 1950s was a particularly promising moment for them. The Russians' propaganda success in launching a space satellite, Sputnik, in October 1957; a proliferation of social criticism by intellectuals and journalists; and weakness in the economy all contributed to a strong showing by Democratic liberals in the 1958 elections. Jack Kennedy was what the liberals in the Democratic party then needed, a promising presidential candidate. And he was also what his father had taught him to be: a winner. He proved that fact again during his own 1958 campaign for reelection to the Senate. The campaign ran efficiently under the control of professionals and the nominal headship of his brother Ted, then a twenty-six-year-old student at the University of Virginia, the law school his brother Bob had attended. The margin of victory over Vincent Celeste was 875,000 votes, the largest of any senatorial race that year and the largest in his state's history. Jack won 74 percent of the popular vote. (Several new Democratic senatorial candidates also won in 1958, some with the financial support of the Kennedy family.) Still, other Democrats probably had a stronger claim on the 1960 presidential nomination: Hubert Humphrey, the stalwart liberal Minnesota senator; Lyndon Johnson, the moderate Senate majority leader; perhaps even Adlai Stevenson, the engaging intellectual who twice ran against the unbeatable Eisenhower. How, then, did Kennedy emerge as his party's candidate in 1960?

In retrospect most people think of Jack Kennedy as a liberal. However, some historians still question that label; they question not so much whether he set out either half-consciously or expediently to become a liberal, but whether he had liberalism at all in his heart. That is doubtful. But by 1963 the South derisively and angrily termed John Kennedy a liberal; big businessmen denounced him as one; the press increasingly praised him for being one; and though he had opposed giving the vote to eighteen-year-olds, young people of visionary bent perceived him as a strong liberal idealist. The swift-moving history of the late fifties and early sixties carried him along, shaping him into a liberal whatever his own reservations. After his assassination in 1963, Kennedy was considered even more progressive as the Great Society and the Vietnam War brought the liberal domestic agenda and the liberal Cold War to their inescapable conclusions.

The word *liberal* has probably had an even more meandering and inconsistent past than most other political terms in popular currency, but its present implications have some clarity. Everybody believes in the improvement of life, but liberals believe in it as a relentlessly programmatic task. To this end they trust in law, administration, technology, and both social and pure science. Liberals are numerous within the professions that employ these tools: teachers, journalists, scientists. They are capable of both indignation and sentimentality. Yet they dislike popular emotions—chauvinistic, xenophobic, or greedy—that may seek gratification in politics; instead, they respect the cold temper and methodology of science. Liberals favor greater egalitarianism, a modest leveling of income, certainly the eradication of poverty and racial injustice. Liberals of the late 1950s insisted that Americans, asleep in their suburban bedrooms, must awaken to a quickened activity in economics, in education and culture, in social services, and in military and foreign aid. John Kennedy, no clear partisan of any ideology, was by temperament exactly suited to speak for the energies that liberals wanted to release.

In the late 1950s as the Soviet industrial growth rate appeared to outstrip that of the United States, national economic growth was an unquestioned goal. Reports by the Rockefeller panel repeatedly called for growth. Insofar as ecological concerns had any place in all this, they were for the scientific disposition of resources in the service of industrial progress. A chief Kennedy White House adviser, Walt W. Rostow, published *Stages of Economic Growth: A Non-Communist Manifesto* in 1960. His objective was for the West to foster worldwide growth in order to demonstrate to the uncommitted third world the superiority of capitalism. The nation, Rostow said, should look on the Soviet system as a business rival.

After the success of Sputnik, Jack Kennedy was one of the first public figures to stimulate the great national debate about the failure of American schools to train their students for a comparable technical and scientific feat. The Kennedy family members, though never scholarly, were consumed by self-improvement and had addressed their own anxieties in much the way the nation was now doing: through a perfectionist self-questioning that has ridden American civilization since its sectarian religious beginnings. That was how Kennedy had been raised. That was the tone of his campaign for president. By now the campaign had plenty of momentum from the Pulitzer Prize–winning best-seller, from the horse race for the vice-presidential nomination in 1956, from the landslide reelection in 1958, and most of all, from the calls for national greatness that increasingly sounded forth from the young Massachusetts candidate for president.

I I I

On the Hustings

IN EARLY 1960 a newspaperman asked President Eisenhower why "in view of the international prestige at stake," we were not pressing to match the Soviet Union in space. The president asked the reporter to begin his question again. "I said, in view of the international prestige at stake . . . " "Is it?" interrupted Eisenhower. "Isn't it?" responded the reporter. "Not particularly, no," replied the chief executive. That attitude went counter to the growing liberal mentality of the time, which exalted energy and activity, especially if generated by the state. And it was conservatism of a kind to be equally distinguished from the nationalist anticommunism of the right; it embodied a determination to measure what is really necessary in national policy over the long stretch, as opposed to what brings the quick ideological and patriotic gratifications of victory. The fatherly Eisenhower, seventy-one in 1960 and unworried about the missile race with the Russians, clashed with the young Kennedy, in his early forties, who with no specific program seemed to make sheer motion a program on its own.

After Sputnik streaked the late night skies in October 1957, Eisenhower actually cut defense spending. "A deterrent," he patiently explained to Congress, "has no added power, once it has become completely adequate for compelling the respect of any potential enemy." But in the later years of the Eisenhower administration, liberals were warning of Soviet superiority over the United States in nuclear weaponry.

The journalistic voice of liberalism, *The New York Times* editorial page, announced in the autumn of 1957 that we were in a "race for survival," that a "feeling of emergency grips the people of the free world . . . our people will not hesitate to make whatever sacrifices are needed." The paper urged a crash program to "assure our superiority in missiles." The liberal Governor Nelson Rockefeller of New York called for both fallout shelters and a resumption of the nuclear testing, which Eisenhower, who preferred a test ban treaty, had stopped in 1958. The Rockefeller Brothers Fund Report of 1958, prepared under the direction of Henry Kissinger, then known as a liberal, argued that a nuclear stand-off required constant improvement in our deterrent force. The report's call for a civil defense program implied an active engagement of the population in the strategy of deterrence, a very deliberate and continued commitment of the national will. In 1960 Eisenhower created a President's Commission on National Goals that issued similar alarms in *Goals for Americans,* published that fall. The television newscaster Howard K. Smith remarked that if Kennedy had not been busy elsewhere, people would swear he had written the document.

Such reports portrayed a country in quest of a fresh sense of national purpose. The immediate cause for worry was the Soviet scientific advances and Premier Nikita Khrushchev's visit to the United States in 1959 when he scared many Americans by his confidence that his country would outdistance theirs. All this ran contrary to the confidence bred in the United States by the defeat of the Great Depression and the Axis powers. As one historian has put it, Americans were worrying that "history might be running the wrong way," that despite the problems the Soviet Union was having in Hungary and East Germany, the Soviet society seemed more purposeful than the American. The beneficiary of this national consensus over "drift" was John Fitzgerald Kennedy. The mood of the nation was belligerent. Communism must be challenged, not merely contained. And Kennedy managed, especially in his television debates with Richard Nixon, to sound more urgent and eager for combat, forcing his opponent into the role of defending the apparent passivity of the Eisenhower years. Kennedy, so it appeared, would be the more likely candidate to seize the initiative against the Soviets.

American educators, including liberal pressure groups like the National Educational Association and the American Association of Graduate Schools, were among the proponents of defense spending. They argued that such spending should go directly into scientific and technological research, and in nurturing the academy, it would indirectly profit the social sciences and the liberal arts as well. Self-interest conformed perfectly with conviction. Liberal academicians, including the professoriate that had entered the Central Intelligence Agency in its early years, were dedicated anticommunists of a global Wilsonian vision. They believed, moreover, in every kind of technical and scientific progress, embracing it for its practicality and for the critical, skeptical intelligence that they identified with it. They perceived right-wing conservatives as mentally self-indulgent, prone to the emotional pleasures of a rhetorical, chauvinistic anticommunism and with little taste for the careful tasks attendant upon maintaining a geopolitical strategy. In his presidential campaign John Kennedy adopted many demands that liberals of the time were urging on him, most notably an educational program that would strengthen intellect and widen ambitions.

A 1960 campaign book carrying Kennedy's name, *The Strategy of Peace*, insisted that the nation "must regain the ability to intervene effectively and swiftly in any limited war anywhere in the world." Cold War Democratic liberalism, originally not much more than responsive to specific threats of Communist expansion in Greece, Berlin, and Korea, now seemed restless for incessant global activity. Our policy had been defensive; Kennedy and the liberals threatened to set things in motion.

Yet the new posture of liberalism had evolved out of its immediate past—and would further evolve into a future liberal politics that would question the very presumptions on which the Cold War had begun. That continuity is an elusive matter of intellectual and moral tone. From the beginning of the postwar confrontation with the Soviet Union, especially the measured terms of that confrontation as George Kennan proposed them, most liberals had spoken for the virtues of sobriety, intellectual discipline, and a precise and nearly emotionless calculation to be the proper bases of international policy. They despised McCarthyism not only for the most obvious moral reasons but also because it was a spasm of fear and anger. Much of their articulate opposition to racism was actually an intellectual contempt for it. Thus the liberals could at once reject the strident anticommunism of the right because of its emotionalism and at the same time desire an intensified anticommunist foreign policy for the demands it would make on the nation's resources and character. On the one side, then, this view of foreign policy looked to activism and engagement; on the other, it looked to restraint of emotions. Specifically this attitude was working toward a recognition, repugnant to the right, that communism abroad was not a monolith but a diversity of local movements contributory to a policy in Moscow that in turn expressed a diversity of motives—ideological, nationalist, offensive, and defensive. Cold War liberalism, in fact, in its conviction that it should be the intellectual constraint of primitive chauvinism, was unwittingly preparing to argue itself out of its own militant premises. The undoing of liberalism would come in Vietnam—a war Kennedy helped along its wayward course—when many liberals were unable to argue convincingly that Vietnamese Communists were a mere creature of an international Communist movement or, in default of that argument, were unable to give some other reason for our continuing the conflict.

Kennedy himself knew much about the complexity of communism. By 1957 he had decided that "underlying revolutionary conditions" had "lost" China, not the Truman State Department. In 1951 he denied the possibility of bringing poor countries away from communism; but two years later he complained of cutting funds for the United Nations programs of technical assistance and children's relief. By 1958 he was a friend to a variety of programs of economic foreign aid. His call in 1957 for trade with Poland implied a sense that the world behind the Iron Curtain was not a bloc but a plurality. In 1960 he spoke repeatedly of the split between Communist China and the Soviet Union, intending to embarrass his foe Vice President Nixon, who had often spoken of a unified Communist world, unvarying in its evil. During his presidential administration he took bold steps to play on the diversity of nation-state identities in eastern Europe. In his fight for the Trade Expansion Act of 1962, for instance, he asked that his discretionary tariff powers be extended to deal with Eastern European countries. In response to favorable economic treatment, Romania refused to take sides in Chinese-Soviet disputes and initiated a trade pact with China, ended the practice of using Russian names for buildings and streets, and signed contracts with western powers to build a large steel foundry.

The liberal call for a new energy in foreign policy was contributing to a public questioning of the health and identity of the national character. In part that is because Americans have customarily perceived their country not as a given that had originated in an ancient, hidden past but as a construct, put together from one moment to the next and dependent therefore upon the excellence of the constructing. The virtues that Americans have most prized are workmanlike: industry, adaptability, self-mastery; and Americans have looked upon themselves as they have upon their country, as acts of construction. Joseph Kennedy was a product of this viewpoint. His shaping of the Kennedy family is a remarkable episode in American history.

The launching of Sputnik, which triggered much of the national anxiety of the late 1950s, quickened a national self-examination. The Russian superiority suggested that our schools were inadequate to train scientists and technicians to be equally proficient, inadequate especially to school young Americans in diligence and an appetite for achievement. Previously, conformity had been a topic among the more widely read social critics. Now it seemed that conformity within the middle classes might be an explanation of why American youth lacked the will and resilience to match the Soviet success. The nation appeared to be failing in the very virtues that it most prized as its foundation and its proper object. And it was the liberal rather than the conservative temper that was the readier to concern itself with the kinds of excellence that were at issue.

Most of all, the sluggish economy injured the Republican party in the elections of 1958, connecting popular material self-interest to the liberal ethos of energy and reform, and it would continue to undermine the Republicans during their remaining two presidential years. The Eisenhower administration discovered, or inherited, the means to prevent depression, but that is quite different from stimulating steady growth. Also, the Republicans were presiding over a paradox of inflation and repeated recession that accompanied a growth rate probably smaller than the rates in western Europe and the Soviet Union. Meanwhile, robust productivity created labor surpluses that the economy was not expansive enough to reabsorb, as well as increasing the demand for social programs hungry for the tax receipts that a more flourishing economy could have provided.

Democrats, including Senator Kennedy, blamed the problems on the inaction of Treasury Secretary George Humphrey. But it was the total structure of the economy that should justly have carried the blame. The larger corporations had reached the economic condition of oligopoly. Large firms dominating one sector of the economy would forswear the energetic but risky work of producing more and selling more, preferring the sedate prosperity that high profits fetched. Their unionized workers, only an elite portion of the whole labor force, had won fairly substantial wages. Consumers paid. None of this, however, promised relief for the unemployed. The rate of unemployment reached as high as 7.5 percent. But most of the protected members of elitist unions were untouched when the recession of 1957, relieved for a while, returned in 1960. Investments in plants and equipment actually decreased by late in the decade to one eighth of the commitment European economies were making in proportion to population.

The Eisenhower administration, unlike the Republican party today, had little connection with the rightist ideologies, the evangelical conservatives, or the cultures and subcultures sustaining them. Its rooting was in the solid business community that had long been a Republican province. The administration had scant means or will to challenge the comfortable arrangements that big business had established for itself. Business remembered the Great Depression as nervously as the rest of the population remembered. Business therefore was defying the usual assumption that it will go for whatever policies offer a boom economy. At this time it was the liberals who pressed for economic growth, just as they pressed for growth in education, in the implements of foreign policy, in the nation's enterprise, and in ambition as a whole.

There were three recessions under President Eisenhower. And attacks by Republican conservatives on the union shop, under which a union required membership is a condition for holding a job, worsened their party's standing in the labor movement. Therefore, getting the stagnant economy moving again was a liberal project that Kennedy could easily adopt. He addressed the concerns of the moment from a centrist position, yet his vague but appealing talk about the national interest and goals sounded far more activist. Kennedy's style was suited to a slightly unfocused malaise that demanded not a clear solution but a rhetorical promise of better, more energetic times. And he spoke for a party that was increasing in power as an agent of change. In the election of 1958 the Democrats won a larger success than the party in opposition to the president usually enjoys in a midterm year. The vote supplied Congress with many liberals who were to figure in the politics of the sixties. Older conservatives such as Senators William Knowland, John Bricker, and William Jenner left the national spotlight. It was an important moment in the reshaping of politics.

After Kennedy's wide victory in Massachusetts, Mrs. Roosevelt, like many liberals, resisted his entry into the 1960 primaries. Certainly she was accurate when her newspaper column accused Joe Kennedy of lavishly supporting his son's presidential campaign, but she could not prove that fact. Jack compared her attack to McCarthyism. Beyond that issue was the former first lady's anti-Catholicism, which was no doubt intertwined with her dislike of Joseph McCarthy. The civil libertarian Paul Blanshard and others made cogent claims that parts of Catholic doctrine, or the statements of some prelates, challenge the principles of separation of church and state enshrined in the Constitution. But Jack Kennedy increasingly distanced himself from official Catholicism on as many points as he could, including birth control and aid to private schools. Among Catholic congressmen, Kennedy was long one of the most circumspect about matters of religion. But Mrs. Roosevelt still had her suspicions. Kennedy must have been furious when she told the Associated Press that she was not certain he could keep church and state separate.

What is most remarkable about the Kennedy candidacy is that his fourteen-year record in Congress did not include many recorded votes that would have made him unacceptable to any interested groups. That the upper house compels so many votes accessible to public scrutiny is a reason why it is rare for a senator to be elected directly to the presidency. Kennedy's presentable record was partly a matter of party loyalty and partly a compromise over issues such as civil rights that had not quite reached the public spotlight. Aside from those few but important issues that seemed to reflect independence—the speech on Algerian independence, the votes against high farm subsidies, the St. Lawrence Seaway, and Mayor Curley—his very personality suggested freshness and candor. This American president was the first to possess all the traits that modern Americans envy, while at the same time they profess their allegiance to plainer virtues. Jack Kennedy had good looks and brains, a beautiful and cultured wife, the right education, both charm and wealth—it is poverty rather than wealth that disgusts the affluent and sheltered American public—and a powerful father ambitious for his son. As the political fortunes of Franklin Roosevelt had been strangely advanced when that child of wealth contracted polio and became the child of adversity as well, Jack Kennedy's background provided something of the burdens that can enhance popular sympathy and fellowship with a candidate. He was a Harvard graduate but was also Irish in a state that had long discriminated against the Irish; he was wealthy yet was a political underdog because of his religion.

For all his driven ambition, this suitor for the affections of the national electorate was in his own way outside the politics he pursued. He was no Honey Fitz quick with a song, no FDR radiating goodwill toward someone he had hardly met, no folksy Harry Truman, no Ronald Reagan speaking as though he and his audience had always agreed with each other on everything. He had not been much of a Senate crony, and he had neither established an easy rapport with any one ideological faction nor managed to convince any of a variety of factions that he was of its persuasion. Perhaps childhood sickness, the presence of a dominant father and elder brother, and hours of reading had cultivated an inner life that only at its own will made connections with the outer world. Or perhaps the upper-class education had taken, producing not a genial patroon like Roosevelt but a patrician on a more fastidious and scholarly model.

Yet Jack's temperament, aloof, detached from some accepted values and without illusions, was quite compatible with a manipulation of the electorate. In 1959, for instance, he told a group of Pennsylvanians that if he went into the convention with many delegates and then were denied the nomination, the Democratic party would risk alienating Catholics and losing the election. Such incidents foreshadowed the opportunistic way in which Kennedy would use his Catholicism in the 1960 campaign, and they created an impression of Kennedy as a man in a hurry.

Religion made the 1960 primaries fascinating political theater. In the time of Al Smith's candidacy there was a story that if a Catholic were president, the Pope's forces would dig a channel under the Atlantic Ocean for a new Vatican City in the Mississippi Valley because Rome was overcrowded. Other stories had Jesuits putting cardinal red drapes in the White House, buying strategic land overlooking West Point and Washington, D.C., and inscribing rosaries on the dollar bill. Such stories came out of a more primitive American past. A typical national joke in the more tolerant times of 1960 was that the Statue of Liberty would be renamed "Our Lady of the Harbor." Kennedy worked, as he had in the 1956 convention, to turn the issue of religion to his advantage. He brought it up repeatedly, raising the issue of bigotry in such a way as to put even nonbigots on the defensive, as though any vote cast against him for any reason would lead the media to label his opponents as bigots.

The first real match came in early April against Minnesota's Senator Hubert Humphrey in Wisconsin. The state's voters learned about Kennedy and PT-109 and heard friendly speeches from his whole family. The Kennedy forces also mailed anti-Catholic literature to Wisconsin Catholics, a trick reminiscent of Mayor Curley's gubernatorial campaign in Massachusetts, when supporters seeking to incite the Catholic vote burned crosses on hills overlooking Boston in imitation of the Klan. Kennedy money bought a plane, the *Caroline*, that gave Jack more mobility than Humphrey had.

Kennedy's victory in the Wisconsin primary was inconclusive, however, because the number of Catholics in that state was proportionately larger than in the nation as a whole. The critical primary came in West Virginia on May 10. Here both candidates campaigned strenuously. Humphrey, concentrating on economic and social issues, sought identification with the voters by drawing on his experience with poverty in the Depression and his memories of Franklin Roosevelt. He frequently spoke in front of a giant picture of FDR. Kennedy offered the voters an interstate highway and a brisker economy. That the family had the help of Franklin D. Roosevelt, Jr., was a coup. With his stentorian voice ringing out in the manner of his father, he evoked the very presence of the beloved president. And perhaps it was not identification with a candidate that voters were responsive to but the air of easy confidence and the promise of leadership that the upperclass, handsome Kennedy—like FDR—could project. The campaign sometimes became despicable. FDR, Jr., asked why Humphrey had not served in World War II: the Minnesotan in fact had been turned down for medical reasons. Kennedy money again flowed. For years it had been going to the campaigns of receptive West Virginia Democrats, and in 1960 sheriffs were offered cash payments said to average $1,000. Kennedy money also arranged the position of candidates' names on the state's complicated ballots. As Harry Truman would later remark, "Joe thought of everything. Joe paid for everything." Frightened by early polls showing he was trailing because of anti-Catholicism, the candidate met the religious question head on—and milked it for all it was worth. No one had questioned his religion, he orated, when he spent two years in veterans' hospitals; no one had questioned his brother's religion before Joe died in a mission over Germany. "Make it clear," advised Sorensen, "that you are a victim of

. . . bigotry by always so stating in passive tense, 'I have been called' . . . 'it has been suggested that' . . . 'people are being asked to vote against me because.'" At some of their candidate's appearances, Humphrey's supporters played Protestant revival humans like "Give Me That Old-Time Religion." Humphrey might have had a substantial complaint if he had known that Cardinal Cushing was calling priests throughout the state on Kennedy's behalf.

Kennedy won 61 percent of the vote. It was plain that whatever strength anti-Catholicism still possessed in American politics, neither it nor anything else was going to keep the nomination from him. After the West Virginia vote Chicago Mayor Richard Daley gave his support, and Kennedy coerced Governor Michael DiSalle of Ohio by threatening to endorse his party opponents in the state primary.

At the Democratic National Convention in Los Angeles, Senator Eugene McCarthy of Minnesota, who had no great love for Kennedy, more than filled the hopes of Stevenson's supporters with his nominating speech: "Do not reject this man who made us all proud to be called Democrats." Kennedy coldly observed that Stevenson seemed to want to be appointed president. But Stevenson's proud personal distance from the manners of popular politics gave him something in common with Kennedy, and Arthur Schlesinger, Jr., has suggested that the style he introduced to the party may have prepared the way for that of the younger man. Kennedy won on the first ballot.

John Kennedy's acceptance speech promised a "New Frontier." The phrase may have come from the title of a book in the family library written by Guy Emerson and published in 1920, which celebrated the resources and the future of American democracy. Emerson wrote, "Americanism means that men and women are born to put more into their country than they take out of it." Kennedy at his inauguration said, "Ask not what your country can do for you—ask what you can do for your country." The speech gives few hints of what programs Kennedy had in mind. He said of his opponent Richard Nixon: "We know it will not be easy to campaign against a man who has spoken and voted on every side of every issue." Nixon could have said the same thing just as credibly about Kennedy. The Democratic platform was liberal enough and contained the strongest program of civil rights to date in the history of political parties. In particular it promised a federal employment practices commission empowered to compel nondiscriminatory hiring in interstate business.

The choice of Lyndon Johnson, who had placed second in the presidential balloting, as the vice-presidential candidate startled some contemporaries. Liberals disliked the moderate Johnson, seeing him correctly as a politician who played rough—and incorrectly as an unreflective Southern conservative. (From today's perspective, it is hard to understand why the originator of the Great Society programs was not perceived as a liberal in 1960.) Bobby Kennedy reassured delegates that Johnson would not be the choice. Many liberals who began to count Kennedy within their ranks were therefore stunned at the sudden offer and acceptance.

Robert Kennedy's account of Johnson's addition to the ticket is that the offer had been a courtesy that Johnson was not expected to take up. Perhaps. But this Southern candidate proved essential to Kennedy's victory, and the choice of a Southerner was imperative to balance the ticket. Al Smith ran with a Southern senator in 1928. Johnson, moreover, was known as a superb campaigner, particularly in the rural South, and he was a power in the Senate. Kennedy admiringly perceived Johnson as a "riverboat gambler," a tall Texan in ruffles and a black coat, a pistol and aces up his sleeve, moving gracefully through the saloon of a nineteenth-century Mississippi steamboat. Johnson's leathery maturity went well with Kennedy's youthfulness, while the Texan's background of poverty complemented Kennedy's upper-class past and bearing. Johnson's down-home speeches played well with Kennedy's, which were crisp, slightly abrasive, and a com-

pound of New England and the Ivy League. And Johnson
had the support of business. Richard Nixon had foreseen the
choice.

The dealings with the liberals on the subject were hardball,
like the treatment of Governor DiSalle during the primaries.
Robert may have been meant to act as a buffer against the
kind of liberals with whom the Kennedys were uncomfortable. Burke Marshall, later Robert's associate in the Justice
Department, has recollected that Bobby did not actually oppose Johnson as the vice-presidential candidate. For his part
Jack simply told a reporter, correctly, that Democrats habitually balanced their tickets with a Southerner. He wanted to
win; he accepted Johnson without hesitation.

Norman Mailer has described Kennedy as a young professor absentmindedly detached from his role of candidate.
Johnson, in Mailer's words, was "a political animal, he
breathed like an animal, sweated like one . . . his mind was
entirely absorbed with the compendium of political fact and
maneuver." Johnson's Cornpone Special, as reporters labeled
his campaign train, was a creature of the Southern landscape
and the culture it triumphantly toured. Johnson said he was
the "grandson of a 'federate soldier." He controlled every detail, the height of his rostrum, the playing of "The Yellow
Rose of Texas" the moment he ended his talk, the departure
of the train at the instant of farewell. "God bless yuh, Rocky
Bottom," so one reporter rendered the talk and tone. "Ah
wish ah could stay an' do a little sippin' an' whittlin with yuh.
. . . God bless yuh, Gaffney." A *Chicago Tribune* reporter wired,
"The son of a bitch will carry the South." It was an old-time
style, the style of a populist or a Southern New Dealer, an
echo of a lost rural age but still having its appeal. It would
not, however, appeal to liberals who associated populism with
McCarthyism or racial bigotry. Whoever among the liberals
may have so perceived Johnson were in for some rethinking.

The campaign yielded nothing in the way of a clear divisive

issue. It pitted moderate Republican Nixon against a candidate who could have been put almost anywhere in the Democratic party spectrum to the left of the Southern racists. One journalist for *The New Republic*, which in those days had not yet been invaded by conservatism, thought of the election as "the political equivalent of Burroughs against IBM. . . . Its outcome will depend not on the clash of ideas, but on the neat and accurate adjustment of ratchets, cams, and cog-wheels." "Two peas in a pod," complained another commentator. Lacking a clearly etched program, Kennedy projected an intangible promise of an energetic American future. It is as though his person embodied whatever program he represented. His opponent was solid rather than a glamorous public personality.

In August the unglamorous and unlucky Nixon suffered an infected knee that put off his campaign for two weeks and left him weakened in health for much of the contest. He caught a cold that took his voice away. He kept to a foolish promise to visit every state, wasting time in Alaska that he should have given to the Midwest. His running mate, Henry Cabot Lodge, Jr., lacked political charisma. Eisenhower's planned May summit meeting with Khrushchev collapsed after a U-2 American reconnaissance plane was shot down over the Soviet Union. To make matters even worse, Eisenhower told a reporter that he could not think of any major policy decisions Nixon had participated in as vice president. That Nixon's own pastor, the Reverend Norman Vincent Peale, condemned Kennedy on religious grounds may have gained votes for the Democratic candidate because much of the country was viewing the election as an exorcism, once and for all time, of political anti-Catholicism.

In September Kennedy addressed the religion issue directly before the Greater Houston Ministerial Association. On television he declared to the nation that he opposed federal aid to parochial schools. He was speaking at ease to Americans who did not share his faith. Al Smith had clearly been ill at ease when he was compelled, only once during his campaign, to address the issue. Using explosive gestures to match his words, Smith had behaved as though the issue were a personal attack on him—and perhaps it was at that earlier moment in the nation's history. Kennedy spoke often, directly and disarmingly, to Americans troubled by his religion. "My experience . . . shows it is a matter of great concern," he said. "I am delighted to answer any questions about it. . . . There is nothing improper in discussing it. . . . All questions that interest or disturb people should be answered." While the Catholic press criticized his statement that "for the officeholder, nothing takes precedence over his oath to uphold the Constitution," Catholics, like liberals, had nowhere to go in the campaign. The House Democratic leader Sam Rayburn cheered: "He's eating 'em blood raw! This young feller will be a great president."

The Kennedy campaign was the best that money could buy. It made good use of the voter-interviewing techniques available at the time. Using careful repeat samplings of voter sentiment, the Democrats found that Nixon, not Kennedy, had more popularity with woman voters and that foreign affairs was the Democratic candidate's greatest weakness. For this reason Kennedy's advisers urged him to cultivate an appearance of being tough on communism, particularly in the television debates with Nixon. There Kennedy sharply criticized Nixon for letting Castro draw Cuba into the Soviet orbit, for "losing" Cuba to communism.

Nixon's biggest error turned out to be agreeing to this series of four debates. He did well on television in 1952 when, evoking the name of his dog Checkers, he replied to charges of financial misconduct, and again in 1960 when he had the "kitchen debate" with Nikita Khrushchev in Moscow. But Kennedy was an accomplished debater himself. Television did no service to the substance of the campaign, partly because the television screen made it a clash of images. Nixon was made up poorly for the camera; Kennedy appeared fresh and relaxed. Kennedy projected an image of youth, glamour, and excitement; Nixon seemed drab, almost nondescript. Kennedy spoke to his audience; Nixon, who had been on a debate team, addressed only his opponent, disregarding the audience. It might as well have been a contest between Herbert Hoover and Franklin Roosevelt. The sad Nixon was reminiscent of the image of Hoover drawn and tired, a Hoover who had done little to combat the Depression; the hopeful Kennedy recalled the buoyant Roosevelt.

The majority opinion among the 70 million Americans who watched the events decided that Kennedy had probably won, but one woman shrewdly remarked, "I don't know whether to vote for the man who may do too little or the man who may try to do too much." Oddly, the impression among radio listeners was that Nixon had triumphed. It was appropriate that television ushered in the era which memory selectively diverts from the stream of history and labels the sixties. That era was an immensely public time, a time when events became collective experiences: a civil rights march, an antiwar demonstration; and television, drawing a whole nation to the funeral of a Kennedy or to a moment of violence in Chicago, could create for an instant the illusion that viewers who were separated by thousands of miles were together on the streets.

When Kennedy proclaimed that the time was ripe "to get this country moving again," he was referring principally to improving the national economy and to closing the alleged missile gap. But these goals implied larger matters of national character, strength, and prestige. In sponsoring a good liberal cause, the removal of the loyalty oath provision in the National Defense Education Act, Kennedy argued that the oath would exclude from federal funding people of conscience whose intelligence the country needed in its scientific competition with the Soviet Union. There was no missile gap. But Kennedy offered an intellectually defensible commentary on a real military question when he argued that weapons of massive retaliation, on which the Eisenhower administration had relied, needed the complement of a mobile conventional force.

On the civil rights issue, Kennedy's voting experts warned that he needed more positive appeal if he were to win as many votes from blacks as Democratic presidential candidates normally did. Consequently, in September he began to refer favorably to the Greensboro, North Carolina, lunch counter sit-ins and the general need to give blacks equal access to public facilities. He also promised to issue an executive order forbidding segregation in publicly funded housing. Then a shining opportunity presented itself. When Reverend Martin Luther King, Jr., was arrested for a traffic offense and was sentenced to six months at hard labor in a Georgia penitentiary, Kennedy had the grace to call Coretta King to express his concern. And Robert Kennedy called the judge and convinced him to release King on bond. The Kennedy brothers were acting just a bit in advance of their times, and acting on an issue that had previously been of little interest to them. Joe Kennedy paid for the printing of 2 million leaflets recounting the King episode, which were passed out at black churches the Sunday before the election. Copies of a restrictive lease against blacks and Jews that Nixon had signed on a home he had purchased also circulated widely; in violation of the election law, the Democratic circular carried no return address. In 1957 Kennedy himself signed a deed barring the sale of his Northwest Washington home "to Negroes or any person or persons of the Negro race or blood," but the Republicans could not obtain that document.

Kennedy defeated Nixon by 303 to 219 electoral votes but won by only a shading in the popular vote, which was extraordinarily high. The victor had won his new office by the most tenuous of margins, perhaps stretched by a bit of conniving among Democratic bosses in Illinois and Texas. Nixon quite responsibly refrained from contesting the election. The Democratic gains in the Congress were also somewhat illusory; the House count for the party actually declined by twenty seats.

Why had not Kennedy won by a wider margin? The economy was soft, and the Democrats were still the majority party. Maybe religion had more to do with the vote than social scientists have been able to detect or Americans would like to believe. Or perhaps the Eisenhower era, despite the raggedness of the economy and the troubled consciousness of the previous years, nonetheless still held its gentle sway among the voters.

I V

A New Generation

"IT ALL BEGAN in the cold," Arthur Schlesinger, Jr., has written of that inaugural day, January 29, 1961. Before Kennedy spoke, Robert Frost tried to read a few lines of poetry he had composed for the occasion. Frost had come down from Amherst College where Kennedy had earlier made foreign policy threats. The poem that Frost intended to read suited not only the bellicose poet himself but also the tenor of the new administration as Kennedy's campaign speeches had defined it:

> It makes the prophet in us all presage
> The glory of a next Augustan age
> Of a power leading from its strength and pride,
> Of young ambition eager to be tried,
>
> Firm in our free beliefs without dismay,
> In any games the nations want to play.
> A golden age of poetry and power
> Of which this noonday's the beginning hour.

The snap of sun on snow occluded Frost's vision, and he substituted an equivalent: "Our new world diplomacy has been afraid of its responsibility. The prediction is an era . . . of more confidence in our power and the right to assert it."

Kennedy's inaugural address sustained the tone. The goals were proud. He addressed the people as citizens. He held forth the promise that "a new generation of Americans" would march forth to do battle with "the common enemies of man: tyranny, poverty, disease and war itself." The dedication remains with us now in phrases chiseled in granite. Thousands, perhaps millions, of visitors to Kennedy's grave in Arlington National Cemetery have viewed these phrases: "Let the word go forth from this time and place, to friend and foe alike, that the torch has been passed to a new generation of Americans—born in this century, tempered by war, disciplined by a hard and bitter peace. . . . " Then, at a time when no especially cold wind was burning across the frontiers of the Cold War, came words that fit the sharp chill of the day: "Let every nation know, whether it wishes us well or ill, that we shall pay any price, bear any burden, meet any hardship, support any friend, oppose any foe to assure the survival and the success of liberty. This much we pledge and more. . . . The graves of young Americans who answered the call to service," Kennedy said, "surround the globe." The speech played to the conviction, as measured by polls, that Americans overwhelmingly ranked foreign policy as the nation's primary problem. Ted Sorensen, who wrote most of the speech, came up with the now famous exhortation: "And so, my fellow Americans: ask not what your country can do for you—ask what you can do for your country." Despite their familiarity, the words still carry the dignity of serious expression. A young black man, James Meredith, heard the speech and decided the next day to apply at the all-white University of Mississippi. Yet only as an afterthought had Kennedy inserted a phrase about defending human rights "at home" as well as abroad.

The inaugural is an elegant piece: its manner far above the standard for political oratory, crisper than the orotund style of the early years of the republic, firm and edged in its contrast to the flaccid pleasantries of twentieth-century American political addresses. In sharp contrast to the style of Ronald Reagan, Kennedy's speech established no cozy intimacy with the audience, it offered a promise not of effortless comfort but of difficulty, and its version of standing tall implied that only sacrifice can bring honor. But what sacrifice, and to what end? Although a credible exercise in style, the speech lacked concreteness. It represented not a program but a moral temper and a conviction—rooted in the American past, in mid-century liberalism, and in the upbringing of a Kennedy—that life is to be a mastery of external problems and personal faults. The ultimate subject of the speech is its author or its speaker: it reads like the projection upon outward events of the private war of self-conquest that put the Puritans to building their pious commonwealth in New England or the twice-born Ohio Valley evangelicals to fighting slavery. Lacking a specific issue, it initiated a time when issues would acquire a vocabulary mingling moral anger with guilt-driven introspection. A rhetorician has claimed that the youthful Kennedy, by associating with the octagenarian poet and by his references to the early days of the republic, "sought to pull over himself the mantle of the Founding Fathers." The passing of "the torch" evoked the ancient olympics; Biblical words and phrases like "writ," "the trumpet," and "split asunder" were also meant to suggest maturity. Certain words, like the repeated "citizen," are venerable, bringing to mind classes in civics or memories of Pericles' funeral oration or the civilization of the ancient Romans, who did more to advance and elevate the idea of citizenship than any other people. The inaugural also managed to invoke the presidencies of Washington, Jefferson, Lincoln, and Franklin Roosevelt. The House Democratic Speaker Sam Rayburn pronounced the speech the best since Lincoln's in 1864.

The Kennedy administration was to be brief—two years and ten months from the trumpet summons of the inaugural to the muffled drums and caissons marching slowly up Pennsylvania Avenue in November 1963. It is a foreshortened story of beginnings and promises, an administration virtually devoid of political corruption and tawdry appointments to high office. Were the hopes raised by the inaugural ultimately fulfilled? Was there substance behind the glittering style? Was the New Frontier's foreign policy a beckoning horizon or an armed border?

Two days after the election Kennedy appointed Ted Sorensen as his special counsel, Pierre Salinger as his press secretary, and Kenneth O'Donnell as his appointments assistant. Like Kennedy himself, who was forty-three, all were young men, Sorensen the youngest at thirty-two. Known as shrewd political planners, they were really shrewd improvisers like most presidential aides, but they brought considerable Washington experience to their jobs. Salinger was probably the least influential of the group, but he persuaded Kennedy to hold press conferences on television so that he could communicate directly with the public. Although he always got along well with reporters, Kennedy looked over their heads and into the cameras when he answered their questions. The American people heard and saw more of Kennedy through these conferences than they had of any other president, and his knowledge and wit set a high standard. That his popularity rating never fell below 59 percent during his presidency was largely due to the press conferences, which almost every American witnessed at one time or another. Preparing for these conferences kept Kennedy informed about a range of government matters and helped to maintain his reputation for being au courant.

Richard Neustadt, a Columbia University political scientist, advised the president on the transition from the Eisenhower administration. He recommended that Kennedy rely on more than one set of advisers and also to reappoint two hoary Washington figures, J. Edgar Hoover of the Federal Bureau of Investigation and Allen Dulles of the Central Intelligence Agency. In a similar gesture of reconciliation appropriate for a president who had narrowly won office, Kennedy met with Richard Nixon in Florida after the election; later he appointed Nixon's former running mate and Kennedy's opponent in his 1952 Senate race, Henry Cabot Lodge, Jr., as ambassador to South Vietnam.

Kennedy personally chose as many of his new staff as he could. On foreign policy matters, he sought advice from men like toughminded Robert Lovett of Wall Street and the Washington lawyer and Truman confidant Clark Clifford. Close to the press, Kennedy was easily reached by journalists like Joseph Alsop and Walter Lippmann. Most of these men were conservative by temperament, and many of Kennedy's appointments reflected their advice, to the chagrin of liberals. Secretary of State Dean Rusk, a moderate from the South, was an imperturbable administrator chosen by Kennedy so that the president himself could shape foreign policy. Secretary of Defense Robert McNamara, the newly appointed head of the Ford Motor Company, tried to streamline the Pentagon. The cost-effective executive, once a teacher at the Harvard Business School, "really runs, rather than walks," even "running up and down the escalator steps," one journalist has remembered. Kennedy chose the Wall Street Republican Douglas Dillon as Secretary of the Treasury and the conservative William McChesney Martin as chairman of the Federal Reserve Board, but he balanced those two appointments with that of Walter Heller as head of the Council of Economic Advisers. Heller was a liberal who favored either tax cuts or an increase in domestic spending as alternative stimulants to the economy.

Few committed liberals won high appointment: they were too ideological, too earnest, too emotional, too talkative, and too dull for Jack Kennedy. Adlai Stevenson was shunted out of the way to New York City as Ambassador to the United Nations. Chester Bowles, who in the opinion of Kennedy activists was moralistic, irresolute, and given to elaborate explanations and argument as perhaps befitted a former publisher of the *Encyclopedia Brittanica,* lasted as Undersecretary of State for only a year. Though he was insistent and independent in his advocacy of a leftward turn in policy, his troubles apparently stemmed from a clash between his ponderous manner and Kennedy's clipped style. The historian Arthur Schlesinger, Jr., served as a White House adviser and wrote a towering memorial for the fallen president, *A Thousand Days,* published less than twenty months after Kennedy's death. The first Italian-American and the first Polish-American ever to achieve cabinet status were appointed by Kennedy: Anthony Celebrezze in 1962 headed the Department of Health, Education, and Welfare and, in 1963, John Grenouski became Postmaster General. Trustworthy centrists won other cabinet places: Abraham Ribicoff of Connecticut was Kennedy's first Health, Education, and Welfare; Luther Hodges of North Carolina became Secretary of Commerce; and Arthur Goldberg was appointed Secretary of Labor. Orville Freeman took over the Department of Agriculture, which to the Kennedys was the most mysterious of all realms. Robert Kennedy had to fit in somewhere, and his father got his way when Bobby became attorney general. The appointment was a good one—and nepotism pure and simple. McGeorge Bundy of Harvard and Walt Rostow of M.I.T., who became important White House foreign policy advisers, might be described as hardline liberals. Even Kennedy found Rostow somewhat brash, calling him the "Air Marshall" for his propensity to advocate bombs as answers to complicated troubles abroad. But Rostow was also a spokesman for peaceful competition with communism, and his emphasis on economic development completed the compound of toughness, progressivism, and trust in expertise that would crystallize in time as the style of the Kennedy circle in foreign policy.

From the start the new administration was oriented toward foreign policy. In this century it has been normal, though not inevitable, for global events to give greater visibility to the presidency, and Kennedy had a particularly close identification with the country's international presence.

The generation that came to office with Kennedy was schooled in wartime, as the inaugural address indicated. The people of that generation knew something about the virtues of getting things done with dispatch, the usefulness of making up rules as you go along; they had seen obstacles yield to force, and they had tasted the pride of victorious American power. Now they were exposed to new techniques: television was annihilating distance and time; there were a lightening and quickening of technology such as obtains in Ian Fleming's James Bond novels, which Kennedy relished. In spite of the violence, Fleming's stories involved more than an arrogant practitioner of secret war. They were early efforts in a spy genre that looked beyond a time when militant westerners had resolved all the details of international politics into confrontations between a free world and a solid Communist bloc. The characters in a Fleming story act for larger forces, but these forces are shadowy and shift from one tale to another. James Bond himself is armed with light, dazzling mechanical devices that evoke the increasingly sophisticated technological world of the Cold War. This understanding of power and politics found a presidential spokesman in a war hero of an elite service, a motorized sea cavalry, who wanted an advanced and mobile military. Kennedy's goals must have sharpened the hunger for activity that had made liberals restive in the later years of the Eisenhower administration. One general recalled that Kennedy "made me gather up all [the weapons] we had that might be used for guerrilla warfare. There were about twenty weapons . . . the most recent of them was something that had been invented in 1944. This was 1961."

This activism, distinguishing itself from Eisenhower's refusal to be rushed, was also distinct from the simple anticommunist militancy that the right favored and that the liberals dismissed as self-indulgent. Kennedy once said that it was a "simple central theme of [his] American foreign policy to support the independence of nations so that one bloc cannot gain sufficient power to finally overcome us." He also observed "It is a dangerous illusion to believe that the policies of the United States, stretching as they do worldwide, under varying and different conditions, can be encompassed in one slogan or one adjective, hard or soft or otherwise." The activity that the administration favored was not some gigantic flexing of American might against communism. It was defter, more alert, more intricately involved in the economic and social and political diversity of the regions where this nation sought an influence. The Peace Corps, whose volunteers would compound moral vision with practicality and technical expertise with the arts of friendship, was as exemplary of what the administration was after as was the other well-known corps of Kennedy volunteers, the Green Berets. A world to be balanced and rebalanced invites an activity more extensive and exact than a world to be remade once and for all.

In their desire to renovate the military into a swifter and more various instrument for use in world politics, Kennedy and McNamara were following Generals Maxwell Taylor and Matthew Ridgway, who were against a primary reliance on a nuclear deterrent. The United States, said Taylor, should be able to fight two and a half wars at one. This unusual general returned to Washington in 1961 as an important White House adviser. He was a liberal's general, a scholar who spoke several languages and wrote several books. In *The Uncertain Trumpet* (1959) he argued against dependence on strategic nuclear weapons, reasoning that tactical nuclear weaponry would produce little fallout of danger to civilians. He was a combination of the fighter, the seasoned critic of force, and the technician.

The counterforce strategy, announced by President Kennedy in 1961, prepared our missiles for strikes not at enemy cities but at missile bases. Apparently McNamara was sincere in preferring this strategy as more humane than a policy aiming weapons at civilians, but it gravely alarmed the Soviet Union, which considered it offensive rather than defensive.

Kennedy's most distinctive military interest was in the Special Forces, or Green Berets. If Peace Corps volunteers were supposed to be soldiers of peace, the Special Forces were projected as the peace corpsmen of war. An early plan for training them proposed that troops parachuting into Hungary be able to discuss the principal Hungarian poets and know the correct words for romance (James Bond—whose name was suggested to the author by the name of an expert in ornithology—is an expert lepidopterist). The president, who had the nation's remaining PT boats routed to Vietnam, offered ideas for equipping the Green Berets. In one instance he suggested using sneakers instead of heavy combat boots; when he was told that bamboo spikes could rip through the sneakers, he recommended reinforcing them with flexible steel innersoles. Restraint might be the hard part in any balance with resoluteness, and President Kennedy's fear of appearing weak could tempt him to overreact.

Can it be fairly said that the Bay of Pigs invasion of Cuba had been forced upon Kennedy during his first months in the White House? In the Eisenhower years the CIA had prepared an invasion force that it hoped would spawn a Cuban uprising against the Communist dictator Fidel Castro. Some 1,400 Cuban refugee guerrillas awaited orders on a coffee plantation in the mountains of Guatemala. During the campaign Kennedy had been a hardliner on Cuba, implicitly suggesting that the Eisenhower administration allowed Cuba to go Communist. Conservative commentators applauded him. Some liberals who learned of the invasion plan were opposed to it: Senator William Fulbright, chairman of the Senate Foreign Relations Committee; Roger Hilsman of the State Department; George Kennan, the liberal architect of the containment policy; Arthur Schlesinger, Jr.; and Chester Bowles. Dean Rusk apparently opposed the invasion but never got around to saying so.

Kennedy listened to other advisers. McNamara, a technocrat austere in conscience and statistical logic, was too impressed by the computerized thinking of the CIA, which demonstrated that the invasion would succeed. The Joint Chiefs of Staff were inarticulate, rating the chance of success as "fair" but not specifying that that term really meant "poor." The Chiefs had a clean record of favoring all belligerent actions. The Navy Chief, Arleigh Burke, was an enthusiastic proponent, and his reputation for being a courageous man of war gave him cachet with the Kennedys. The Pentagon's Roswell Gilpatric and Paul Nitze, Henry Fairlie observes, "seemed like hardened missiles . . . called from the Cold War silos in which they had been emplaced a decade earlier." Allen Dulles of the CIA rated the venture as having the same chance of success as the Eisenhower administration's successful intervention of 1954 in Guatemala. Faced with the seemingly insoluble problem of not knowing how to disband the guerrillas, Kennedy in April 1961 gave his approval for the Cuban assault.

Whatever could go wrong did go wrong. The landing spot, surrounded by swamps that choked off the retreat to the mountains that the plan projected in case of trouble, happened to be familiar to Castro because it was his favorite fishing spot. Little grasslike squiggles on the maps meant nothing to most of the planners; one CIA participant, like practically any boy scout, could recognize them as symbols for swamps. "I don't think we fully realized," muses Schlesinger, "that the Escambray Mountains lay *eighty miles* from the Bay of Pigs, across a hopeless tangle of swamps and jungles." One road they believed to be important actually ended in a swamp. Also, no one seemed to realize that Castro had an army of at least a quarter million troops well equipped by the Soviet

Union. Using old United Fruit Company freighters, the invaders placed all their radio equipment and much of their inadequate munitions in a single boat, which got blown up; a number of planes intended for air cover arrived an hour late because time zones had not been well coordinated. Coral reefs ripped the hulls of some craft.

What Kennedy did right at the Bay of Pigs—about the only thing he did right but the most important—was to show restraint at a critical point: he refused to send major United States air support. "Most conspicuous" of the Kennedy presidency, writes the conservative critic Hannah Arendt " . . . were the extremes to which he did *not* go." Perhaps it was real wisdom that kept him from a proud continuation of a futile combat, or possibly it was Adlai Stevenson's ultimatum to resign from the United Nations. Another consideration may have been Khrushchev's announcement, "Cuba is not alone," accompanied by a hint of Soviet retaliation, possibly in Berlin or Southeast Asia, against any direct action on the part of the United States. In any event, Castro defeated the invaders and took many prisoners whom he later traded for medical supplies and farm equipment. Former President Eisenhower lamented that Kennedy had not taken the opportunity to invade Cuba: the Bay of Pigs, he said, should be called a "Profile in Timidity and Indecision." Third world nations were deeply shocked; after the compulsive anticommunism of Eisenhower's Secretary of State John Foster Dulles, they had expected better.

The attempted invasion was misconceived, but it does not deserve to be equated with the Soviet intervention in Hungary in 1956. That was a brutal repression of a popular uprising. The attempt at the Bay of Pigs was conceived as an act of liberation. It was a sincere, albeit naive, conviction at the time, even among government officials who were supposed to be knowledgeable, that people living under Communist regimes were captive populations yearning for rescue. Castro had more political prisoners than the rightest government that preceded him; mass trials and mass executions disposed of dissenters. Despite improvement in the wretched living conditions of the Cuban people, Castro's government deserved condemnation. But the United States also drew criticism in the hemisphere by being suspicious of popular movements that aimed for the redistribution of wealth, by dictating Latin American internal politics by force, and by favoring oligarchies that keep their people in poverty.

Whether the Kennedys later moved against Castro by ordering his assassination is a question as yet unanswered by the archives. Certainly the CIA was trying to do in Castro, but CIA efforts had begun two years earlier in the Eisenhower administration, which recruited gangsters to kill Castro. The Kennedys authorized sabotage and commando raids against Cuba in Operation MONGOOSE, but John McCone, whom Kennedy chose to replace Allen Dulles as head of the CIA, claims he never knew about the assassination plots. McCone, a Republican industrialist, was not the type of man who would supervise killings. There is no evidence that any president knew before Lyndon Johnson, who canceled the program. If Kennedy did know, of course, his own murder by Lee Harvey Oswald was a turnabout of fate, since Oswald was a leftist psychopath who had visited the Soviet Union and organized a Fair Play for Cuba Committee. At any rate the Kennedy administration kept pressure on Castro. A memorandum from Dean Rusk urged the government to "tighten the noose around the Cuban economy and to increase the isolation of the Castro regime from the political life of the hemisphere until the regime becomes a complete pariah." General Edward Lansdale supervised the sabotage of oil refineries and sugar mills, and the CIA provided anti-Castro guerrillas with firearms. European nations were asked not to trade with the island state.

The administration's obsession with Cuba was offset by its

plans for an Alliance for Progress through Latin America, a $10 billion decade-long program of economic assistance. Fulfilling a campaign promise to attempt to "create a Latin America where freedom can flourish," the alliance at Punta del Este in Uruguay in 1961 pledged itself to land and tax reform and economic assistance from the United States, the first such commitment ever made. Economic decline, which had characterized the region in the 1950s, was checked, and substantial progress was achieved in reducing illiteracy. Improvements also came in health benefits and government housing. But no change came in income distribution, nor was there any net transfer of resources or wealth from industrialized to developing countries. The plan never went so far as to abandon right-wing regimes that promised stability, and to that extent it was irrelevant to the situation in Latin America. But Juan Bosch, a leader in the Dominican Republic pushed aside by Lyndon Johnson's marines in 1965, said of the Alliance, "That was the only time the U.S. ever followed a correct policy in Latin America."

The CIA, of course, has been a presence in any number of adventures abroad. But liberals and the Kennedys had a particular affinity for the agency. Founded in 1947 after the demise of the Office of Strategic Services (OSS), the espionage organization had acquired a reputation for leftist sympathies during World War II; the CIA at its conception was a club of scholars and analysts. At least one in ten of the agency's members in the Eisenhower and Kennedy years held a doctorate. Joe McCarthy attacked the agency with abandon, and Richard Nixon labeled it a stronghold of liberalism. In Robert Kennedy's words: "During the 1950s . . . many of the liberals who were forced out of other departments found a sanctuary, an enclave, in the CIA. So some of the best people in Washington, and around the country, began to collect there. One result of that was the CIA developed a very healthy view of Communism. . . . They were very sympathetic, for example, to nationalist, and even Socialist governments and movements." In 1954 the CIA engineered the overthrow of a progressive government in Guatemala, which has suffered since then under a succession of repressive regimes. But one of the agency's operations in the 1950s involved helping the uprising against the Cuban dictator Fulgencio Batista.

President Kennedy shared with CIA officers a background of class and education, along with intellectual curiosity. They were the kind of liberals he could respect, virile and energetic. One designer of the Bay of Pigs was Richard Bissell, impatient, eccentric, brilliant, a sailor and mountain climber who had previously taught economics. This Stevenson Democrat believed that Castro had betrayed a progressive, democratic revolution. Of opponents of Castro like himself, he wrote, "We're the real revolutionaries." Kennedy himself in *The Strategy of Peace,* published early in 1960, placed Castro in the legacy of the liberator Simon Bolivar. By the end of the campaign Kennedy was accusing Castro of turning against the revolution.

The Bay of Pigs turned the Kennedys against the CIA, and Robert Kennedy himself headed the program for building counterinsurgency forces to work against Castro. Robert would later claim that the failure had taught the administration a great deal, generally encouraging caution and keeping the United States from sending a heavy commitment of troops to fight communism in distant Laos. The president came to trust in his own judgment and to rely on balanced sets of advisers, as he did in the Cuban missile crisis of October 1962. He also placed greater reliance on the bureau of intelligence and research (the INR), which was the intelligence arm of the State Department. Roger Hilsman, later Kennedy's Assistant Secretary of State for Far Eastern Affairs, headed the advisory agency. A West Pointer who had led an OSS mission behind enemy lines in Burma, he was among the administration officials who sought a balance between confrontation and restraint in foreign policy. While the

INR drew up some demented schemes for fighting Castro, it also held back the CIA from adventurism, once buying up some contaminated Cuban sugar destined for the Soviet Union. Hilsman also pushed to cut back the CIA practice of subsidizing political liberals who wrote for intellectual magazines like *Encounter* and gave lectures about the iniquity of communism. Hilsman's liberalism reached into the planning on Vietnam: "Just use your troops to protect the people. Then, behind that screen, you have social and political reform, land reform—and very deep reform—education, everything. And then the sea of the people in which Mao says the guerrillas swim like fish will have dried up." Yet, "We were all grossly misinformed about the convolutions, the thickness, the obstacles, that Vietnamese culture represents."

V

At the Brink?

THE BAY OF PIGS and the Kennedy inaugural address together defined an imperial presidency in foreign affairs. Kennedy's summit meeting with Premier Nikita Khrushchev in June 1961, the confrontation over the Berlin Wall that autumn, and the Cuban missile crisis in 1962—all seemed one roll of distant thunder, alarming if not apocalyptic.

At first Kennedy seemed to have learned very little from the Bay of Pigs. That invasion was based on the premise that because communism was totalitarian, the people who lived under it yearned for freedom and would revolt at the first opportunity. The blunder seemed to teach Kennedy the wrong lesson: it firmed his resolve to anticipate—almost to seek, according to some critics—and to be prepared for future encounters. He discounted arguments that building up an arsenal of conventional weapons would itself be provocative and nettle the Soviet Union into doing the same. He encouraged the continuing of efforts to dislodge Castro.

After the Bay of Pigs, he played his next moment on the international stage when he and Khrushchev met in Vienna in June for a summit conference. The Soviet chief had initiated the meeting ostensibly to advance peace; it was an invitation which Kennedy thought world opinion required him to accept, and it would give him an opportunity to gauge his wily opponent. Before he announced his agreement to make the visit, he spoke to the Canadian Parliament on the need to strengthen conventional and nuclear armaments. The Soviet military budget was on the rise, and Kennedy, unlike Eisenhower, was determined to keep up with or outdo the enemy.

Until the mid-1950s the Soviet leaders, always fearful of a German nationalism that had killed millions of their countrymen, demanded a permanent separate status for economically weak Communist East Germany. They feared an eventual allied thrust, led by West Germany in alliance with the NATO powers, that might follow economic and political chaos in East Germany. That collapse could come from the continued flow of East Germans through the passage from East to West Berlin, a migration that included many professionals and skilled young people. The rhetoric of the political leadership of West Germany was provocative, and Soviet spies reported seeing German pilots in planes that carried American nuclear weapons. So Khrushchev threatened to sign a separate peace treaty with East Germany unless the West gave him a secure alternative.

The Soviet Union was defensive and fearful of the West, which had periodically invaded Russian soil. But to the Western allies the brutality of Soviet domination in Eastern Europe blurred any distinction between defensive and aggressive intentions. West Berliners under the shelter of the NATO powers enjoyed a different existence, and they felt obliged to continue that shelter. Khrushchev's plan to make West Berlin a free city under the supervision of the United Nations, East Germans to be denied exit through it, would sever the protective connection with the allies. Khrushchev's posture toward Berlin was confrontational: it had become a "bone" in the Russian throat much as Cuba was in the American throat. The Russian leader tried to put the allies on the defensive; he called Berlin "the testicles of the West. When I want the West to scream, I squeeze in Berlin." The Russians were planning to renounce the original allied plans agreed to at the Potsdam Conference in June 1945. That fate happens to an agreement when a signatory finds it inconvenient or no longer relevant, and the Potsdam accord was becoming irrelevant. But the West perceived Moscow as having written its own rules for Eastern Europe since the end of the war, in contravention of clear understandings, and Khrushchev's threat fit in with everything that the allies detested in Soviet foreign policy.

At Vienna Khrushchev became bombastic about opening the rest of the world for the spread of Communist revolution. Concerning a developing civil war in Laos, where each super-power had been supplying a faction, the two leaders managed to agree on some disengagement. But on the overriding issue of Germany, each went home angry after an exchange of fat-uous generalities about communism and capitalism. Kennedy staked out a clear but not uncompromising position: the West would not abandon West Berlin. Beyond that, he annoyed Khrushchev by indicating his desire to maintain the status quo in the world, not only the inviolability of borders but also of economic systems. The Russian replied according to stan-dard Marxist theory: the world would move his way without resort to force.

Viewed from the West, the Soviet Union seemed (correctly so) to be in a moment of proud assertiveness. Notwithstand-ing the falsity of Democratic claims about a missile gap, the U.S.S.R. had broken triumphantly ahead of the United States in the more sensational objectives of early space programs, most spectacularly in launching the first manned space satel-lite shortly before the summit conference. The Soviets also benefited from the Bay of Pigs fiasco. Robert Kennedy claimed that our refusal to invade Cuba led the Soviet Union to conclude that the new president was weak; this view as-sumes something close to simplemindedness on the part of all parties.

Also important was the public personality of Khrushchev. Though tempering the severity of the Soviet government at home, he was the most verbally truculent of leaders in ad-dressing the capitalist world. His manner suggested an earthy peasant, friendly but tolerating no nonsense, which he alone was competent to define, and quick to instruct, scold, and warn. The very force of his jovial arrogance conveyed the sense that Moscow now had the initiative. But Khrushchev's situation, viewed from inside Soviet realities, did not look so secure. That he had brought some degree of restraint to the continuing institutions of domestic repression after the Stalinist era of terror may have been a political asset; but his concomitant aim of getting goods into the hands of consumers put him at odds with the militarists, led by Frol Kozlov and Mikhail Suslov, over how much of the country's resources should go to the armed services. Possibly he thought that a bloodless victory over the German question could both outflank the chauvinism of his opponents and lessen the need for military spending.

Dean Acheson, Secretary of State under President Truman, as much the patrician as Khrushchev was the peasant, could have commiserated with the Soviet leader in the matter of chauvinist domestic antagonists. Acheson's tenure as Secretary of State epitomizes the experience of liberalism in the early years of the Cold War. Even as he was contributing to the construction of an anticommunist foreign policy so rigid, so broad in its definition of the enemy, that American statesmen ever since have struggled to devise sensible programs within its ideological constraints, conservatives of excitable temperament were assailing him as soft on communism. When Kennedy asked for his advice on the Berlin situation, Acheson still held the same convictions. He viewed the German problem as a "simple contest of wills." His recommendations were to send a division of American troops on the Autobahn through East Germany to Berlin, to declare a national emergency, and to make it plain that, if necessary, we would fight a nuclear war over Berlin. Since there was nothing to negotiate, he argued, there should be no summit conference. (Kennedy wrote in a memo that summer: "I'm somewhat uneasy to have refusal to negotiate become a test of firmness.") The head of the leftist Americans for Democratic Action said in the liberal manner of the time: "The crisis in our affairs is not less serious than that confronting the nation in 1933. Nothing less is at stake than the survival of freedom."

For his part Kennedy thought Khrushchev was using the Berlin crisis to probe Western weakness. On the one hand, he advised canceling a planned but now provocative meeting of the West German Parliament in West Berlin. On the other he asked Congress for a crash civil defense program with bomb shelters, requested estimates of casualties in the event of nuclear war, and told friends and journalists he thought such a war might occur. He also began a multibillion dollar effort to reach the moon, a commitment which suggests he had other expectations of the future. In a speech about Berlin on July 25, 1961, he proposed sharp increases in military expenditures and in the size of the armed forces, including doubled draft calls and a mobilization of 51,000 reserves. "We do not want to fight, but we have fought before," he said. The president was making a military and diplomatic point; his words were harsh, yet even the pacific liberal Chester Bowles of the State Department thought we had to assert our willingness to protect West Berlin with whatever means necessary.

The allies made no unified response. Prime Minister Harold Macmillan of Britain did not want to fight to protect the Germans. France's Charles DeGaulle was content to ignore Moscow while he concentrated on remaking France into a great world power. Chancellor Adenauer was torn between a policy of rejecting concessions and a fear of more fighting on the homeland along with a clear conviction that West Berlin was not worth nuclear war.

Despite his truculence, which included indirect threats to use nuclear weapons if necessary to protect West Berlin, Kennedy left the issue open to compromise and consulted a range of advisers, the majority of whom counseled caution. He realized that the danger of economic ruin in East Germany would push the Soviet Union to the brink. The president's secretary of state thought that he was too eager to negotiate a way out of the crisis. In a remark later retracted, Senator William Fulbright of the Foreign Relations Committee said on a television program that it might be all right if the Communists closed off East Berlin: "I don't understand why the East Germans don't close the border because I think they have a right to close it." Kennedy's reply to a question at his press conference that touched on Fulbright's comments avoided the issue of whether East Germans had the right of free exit. He observed privately that Khrushchev would have to halt the stream of refugees, perhaps by "a wall." He could defend West Berlin, but he could not stop Moscow from putting an end to emigration from the East.

In keeping with his newfound caution about using the power of the military, Kennedy recognized how dangerous the situation in Germany had become. Kenneth O'Donnell has remembered the president's remarking in the course of the crisis, "Before I back Khrushchev against the wall, the freedom of all Western Europe will have to be at stake." When Khrushchev began to build the Berlin Wall, Kennedy apparently responded with relief. He reasoned: "Why should Khrushchev put up a wall if he really intended to seize West Berlin? . . . This is his way out of his predicament . . . a wall is a hell of a lot better than a war."

Yet the Communist act jolted the West. On August 28, 1961, an annoyed President denied a story in that day's *Washington Post* that the closing of the border in Berlin on August 13 had caught the United States by surprise. But evidently it had. According to some people, only Germans could have undertaken the arduous task of constructing a 110-mile wall. The West Berliners needed some belligerent gestures to reassure them that their allies would not abandon them and to warn Khrushchev against future actions. The administration, despite its understanding of the geopolitics of the wall, was of divided disposition, genuinely angered at the Communist act that it perceived as ruthless but that it also perceived as stabilizing. Kennedy sent 1,500 troops along the Autobahn through East German territory to West Berlin, an act that Richard Nixon denounced as an "empty gesture." Yet it was a highly aggressive response to what had been a clearly defensive act. The president also sent Vice President Lyndon Johnson to Berlin where he pledged that American soldiers would defend the city. And to bolster Berliners psychologically, he sent General Lucius Clay, the defiant organizer of the victorious airlift of 1948 and the American high commissioner for Germany at the time. The Berliners considered the general their special friend. Charles Bohlen, however, went along with Clay to discourage the impetuous military man from taking any impetuous action. Walt Rostow suggested that the United States go it alone in Berlin's defense, specifically recalling Marshall Kane's decision in the movie *High Noon*. Kennedy's strident speech on July 25 put Khrushchev under pressure from Russian generals to resume nuclear testing; he did so in August, and the United States followed in September. The next spring the American Starfish nuclear blast lit the Hawaiian night and the Australian skies, and temporarily altered the Van Allen radiation belt.

After many United States and Soviet gestures, both symbolic and concrete, the Berlin crisis finally petered out. On the border American and Soviet tanks once faced each other snout to snout when General Clay challenged the right of the East Germans to restrict Western military movements between the sectors. Once again the Soviets pulled back from confrontation. Kennedy warned Clay against excessive insistence on the details of Western rights. He wired the general about the importance of a "clear impression of determination, calmness, and unity." Clay went home by May 1962. Khrushchev withdrew the deadline for a Western agreement to a separate East Germany in return for continued access to West Berlin. Kennedy had probably shown the greater restraint— or indecision. At one point the Soviets gravely endangered civilian airlines using the Berlin corridor by forcing them into dangerous flight patterns. At home, furious voices on both the right and the left lambasted Kennedy; in Bonn, university students sent him a black umbrella, which since the early days of the Cold War had been a symbol of appeasement, a reference to British Prime Minister Neville Chamberlain's familiar umbrella and his meeting with Hitler at Munich. West Berlin itself went into an economic slump, with many of its residents moving to West Germany. The French leader Claude Monnet, a friend to the United States, complained, "Kennedy is not tough enough."

Kennedy's basic support for West Berlin had never wavered in the face of Khrushchev's brandishing of nuclear weapons. In June 1963 he delivered in that city his famous: "*Ich bin ein Berliner*," "I am a Berliner" speech. The crowd went wild with emotion at the anaphoric refrain "Let them come to Berlin," causing Chancellor Konrad Adenauer to wonder whether another demagogue like Hitler could rule the German people. "There are some," Kennedy proclaimed, "who say that communism is the wave of the future. Let them come to Berlin." He continued: "And there are some who say in Europe and elsewhere, 'We can work with the Communists.' Let them come to Berlin." And one more time: "And there are even a few who say that it is true that communism is an evil system, but it permits us to make economic progress. Let them come to Berlin." And at the end: "All free men, wherever they may live, are citizens of Berlin, and, therefore, as a free man, I take pride in the words '*Ich bin ein Berliner.*'" Kennedy was momentarily contradicting the whole drift of his administration toward détente; it was a lapse in which "the heart had obviously turned the head," according to Herbert Parmet. (When President Ronald Reagan visited the city in 1982, he recalled Kennedy's words, "We in America and in the West are still Berliners, too, and always will be.") Despite the bellicose language, the speech was warranted as a gesture of defiance of the communists; the free part of the city was entitled to an assurance that the West would stand by it. Nevertheless, Chancellor Adenauer perceived Kennedy as something of an appeaser over Berlin and subsequently sided with French President Charles de Gaulle against the United States and Britain in rivalries over European leadership. Kennedy appreciated the stability that grew out of the Berlin Wall and generally avoided the easy propaganda rhetoric it offered. As late as 1986, Dean Rusk called East Berlin "a giant prison camp."

Western Europe, as the Berlin Wall incident dramatized, was no longer digging itself out of the rubble of war. The economy was now throbbing with energy. Kennedy encouraged Britain to enter the European Common Market, but he discouraged plans to give nuclear weaponry to the continental powers. Beyond that, he envisioned a "Grand Design," an integrated military, economic, and political approach, to encourage an improved alliance between the United States and Western Europe. An Atlantic-wide free trade area would bring tariffs down, increase United States exports, and enhance its global strength. If West Germany in particular were to be defended at all costs, it should in return contribute toward maintaining American troops and assisting underdeveloped nations. Kennedy did not wish to bring an economic decline upon his country, but experts disagree about the effectiveness of the president's trade policies.

Kennedy's military strategies in Europe, like the economic and political plans that were to ground and sustain them, never achieved a striking degree of success, but they contain the grandness of vision that is still associated with his presidency. The administration's approach was essentially to substitute flexible response for Eisenhower's reliance on a massive retaliation with nuclear weapons. Kennedy's wish was to maintain control of nuclear weapons while relying on European ground forces to handle serious international problems. Should it become necessary to use nuclear weapons, we might be able to make an antiseptic attack on Soviet military installations instead of waging total nuclear war. The proud de Gaulle would not surrender an independent French nuclear retaliatory force, and with some reason. A land war in

Europe using NATO forces would devastate that continent and leave the American homeland unscathed. And would the United States use nuclear weapons to defend Europe if doing so meant a nuclear attack on American cities?

In mid-1962 President Kennedy offered a plan known as the Multilateral Force (MLF), which would include a fleet of surface vessels armed with Polaris nuclear missiles and manned with NATO troops, including Germans. That every participating nation could veto the weapons' use would leave nuclear deployment effectively under Washington's control. This scheme smacked of American suzerainty and also of the Wilsonian presumption that equated our interests with the cause of Western civilization. In December 1962 Prime Minister Macmillan of Britain met with President Kennedy in Nassau to advance the Grand Design, but de Gaulle's intransigence forestalled any progress. In January 1963 when de Gaulle scuttled American plans by rejecting Britain's entry into the Common Market, the predominant view in Washington was probably not wide of a State Department officer's remark: de Gaulle "is a bastard who is out to get us." No doubt he had grand designs himself, perhaps a reborn Europe under a Charlemagne instead of an Atlantic community. But Kennedy's plan was a bold one, and the administrations that followed his did no better.

Stability in Europe would give Kennedy freedom to tend to the Cold War in the third world. Most administration initiatives took place there: Laos, Vietnam, Cuba, the Alliance for Progress, Africa, and the Peace Corps. The president personally assured the foreign minister of Israel, Golda Meir, that the United States would rush to Israel's support in the event of an invasion—a stronger assurance than any previous administration had offered. The two countries, he explained, had a "special relationship" much like the one between the United States and Great Britain. But the situation in Africa was particularly alarming. In the Congo, Ghana, and Portuguese Angola the Soviets were apparently making advances toward establishing a new Communist frontier, something the United States was determined to prevent.

In Africa, as in Asia, the countries of western Europe were faced with a surging nationalism in their colonies. Congressman John Kennedy had no use for colonialism, claiming that it had held Ireland in bondage for a thousand years. As Senator, he complained that the European powers were aggressively seeking the support of the United States in the preservation of their colonial empires. Kennedy resisted. He believed that Eisenhower's preoccupation with communism in the Middle East, notably Lebanon, and in Northern Africa, notably Egypt, missed the point by not recognizing and dealing with nationalism. In a bid to gain liberal support and to get the administration to see him as the main Democratic presidential contender, he focused on Algeria, making what *The New York Times* called "the most comprehensive and outspoken arraignment of Western policy . . . presented by an American in public office."

After his Algerian speech, influential Africans in Washington sought out Kennedy, for the speech had come at the same time as a revolutionary movement toward independence in the black African nations. He acted in Kennedyesque fashion: he offered none of the conventional bromides about how much capitalism could do for African countries that naturally looked with fascination on the more comparable models in China and in Soviet states. In 1959 Kennedy became head of the Senate Foreign Relations Subcommittee on Africa. In 1959 and 1960 he gave thirteen speeches concerning that continent. Revolution, he warned, was "spreading like wildfire in nearly 1,000 languages and dialects." He proposed an African Education Development Fund. During the presidential campaign he pointed out that the Eisenhower administration had given only 5 percent of its technical assistance aid to African countries. Such comments made their indirect appeal to American blacks.

The most important scene of trouble in Africa came in the Congo and had begun well before Kennedy took office. Hundreds of people were killed in the summer of 1960 as the Belgians tried to hang on to some vestige of their power. Eisenhower refused assistance to Prime Minister Patrice Lumumba, an enormously popular national leader who then persuaded the United Nations to send in a 10,000-man multinational force to try to evict the Belgians. The Soviets sent in planes and trucks to Lumumba, after which President Eisenhower apparently ordered his assassination. Kennedy received intelligence that Lumumba was not a Communist but a nationalist who wanted to use the Russians. Following his election, Kennedy received a long congratulatory message from Lumumba.

In 1961 a new policy, the "Kennedy Plan," involved the strengthening of UN forces to guarantee self-determination for the Congo. The president's brother Edward, back from a fact-finding tour of Africa, recommended Lumumba's release from prison, where a new government had placed him. After weeks of delay and wavering, news came that Lumumba had been murdered, either by native factions or by CIA operatives, even before the president had taken office. Kennedy warned Moscow that unilateral intervention in the Congo would bring "risks of war" and endorsed UN efforts to expel the Belgians. The administration favored a nationalist coalition regime in the hope that it would contain the Soviet Union. But when it appeared that a radical nationalist might take power, Kennedy held back support once again, seeing Africa primarily as a stage for the Cold War.

Throughout his term Kennedy would not allow United States military intervention in Africa on the side of the UN. After the untimely death, or murder, of UN Secretary General Dag Hammarskjöld while on an African mission, the president sent a new ambassador to the Congo, Edmund Gullion, with the aim of allowing each country in Africa "to find its own way" toward forging political coalitions at the center.

However, recurrent civil war in the Congo prevented satisfactory solutions. Ultimately Kennedy supported Hammarskjöld's policies, but the brutality of UN troops made matters difficult.

Elsewhere in Africa, Kennedy proceeded with efforts to maintain good relations with Kwame Nkrumah of Ghana, who had led the Gold Coast colony to independence in 1957. After Lumumba's murder, Nkrumah had moved toward Moscow. But Kennedy, rather than write off the popular leader as he had apparently done with Lumumba, continued to support him. Vast funds were sent, albeit reluctantly, to build a dam on the Volta River, and Kennedy succeeded in keeping Nkrumah neutral. He could do little about the iron rule of Portugal's Salazar in Portuguese Angola.

Kennedy's African record deviates from the antinationalist tendency of the United States in the third world. His penchant was for making decisions at the margin, committing little, and leaving room for escape. In Vietnam this course would be disastrous, but in the countries of revolutionary Africa it got him by.

The Peace Corps was the American agency that had the most enduring effect on Africa as well as on most of the third world. The 100,000 volunteers who have served in the Corps are one of the Kennedy administration's most enduring legacies. Similar ideas of volunteer service long preceded the 1960s: in the work of various missionaries, in resolute Yankees like Tom Dooley, who brought medical advances to southeast Asia, and in a tradition of noblesse oblige on an international scale. If viewed skeptically, the Kennedy volunteers and their successors might seem to be little more than warriors in the Cold War, compounding Americanism and capitalism and containment of communism. In fact, they were road surveyors, nurses, agricultural technicians, engineers, and teachers. These specialties were always at the core of the experience because literacy correlated so well with improved living conditions. Peace Corps members rarely argued for United States foreign policy; but by respecting the cultural integrity of their host countries, they built a goodwill that had undoubted political usefulness. If this was more Kennedy counterinsurgency, it wore a velvet glove. Peace Corps service was in vivid response to his call of the inaugural: "Ask not what your country can do for you—ask what you can do for your country." The Corps, as one historian says, "came to epitomize the idealism and hope that so many young people invested in Kennedy."

Several House and Senate members, including Hubert Humphrey, had been suggesting a Peace Corps for years. Kennedy seized on the idea toward the end of his presidential campaign. He complained that American ambassadors did not know the native languages of their host countries. Then on October 14, 1960, when he went to the University of Michigan campus in Ann Arbor, he discovered 100,000 students waiting to see him—even though his arrival was at about 2 A.M. Tom Hayden, a founder of Students for a Democratic Society, was among the group. "How many of you," Kennedy asked extemporaneously, "are willing to spend ten years in Africa, or Latin America, or Asia?" He urged them to make greater personal effort and sacrifice. The students responded enthusiastically. Kennedy told a staff member he had "hit a winning number." In Pennsylvania later in the month he orated: "We need young men and women who will spend some of their years in Latin America, Africa, and Asia in the service of freedom." The idea of a Peace Corps, which concorded so well with that of a global mission, had its clearest formulation in Kennedy's speech at the Cow Palace on November 2 in San Francisco. He complained of the "ugly American": "Men who lack compassion . . . were sent abroad to represent us in countries which were marked by disease and poverty and illiteracy and ignorance, and they did not identify us with those causes and the fight against them." What developing countries needed was "technical, managerial, and skilled labor." The candidate invoked a "new relationship" between the United

States and developing nations. The Peace Corps would be one answer to that need. It was, said a journalist, the one fresh idea of the campaign.

Sargent Shriver, Kennedy's youthful brother-in-law, directed the Peace Corps with typical Kennedy energy and enthusiasm, and with sensible bipartisanship. He won autonomy for the organization, and *Life* soon reported that the Peace Corps was the "hottest topic on college campuses." There were a few opponents: the Daughters of the American Revolution voted to condemn the new organization, 1,072 to 1; and the *New Republic* said we should send substantial amounts of what really mattered: money. There were compromises: participants were required to take loyalty oaths, and more than one trainee was rejected because of leftist activities. And the Peace Corps was projected as an agency in the struggle with communism, which in no way compromised its integrity in a day when liberals could identify the cause of anticommunism with the cause of democratic progressivism. Shriver made Cold War arguments to Congress and Kennedy in order to secure funding. After meeting with Sekon Touré of Guinea, he told the president the Corps was steering that country away from Moscow.

In general the Peace Corps worked effectively and was successful. Only one in five applicants was accepted, following fairly stringent psychological examination. The Corps had to write its own textbooks and dictionaries in scores of exotic languages: Tshi, Twi, and Hausa, for example. Training programs often lasted from 7:00 A.M. to 10:00 P.M. seven days a week. Congress, however, forced trainees bound for left-leaning Ghana to learn more Marxism than Twi. The Peace Corps actively and successfully recruited blacks at every level. The agency also encouraged women to enroll but dismissed any single female who became pregnant. By 1963 at least 7,000 letters came into Washington every week expressing interest in the organization. Notable participants included Senator-to-be Paul Tsongas of Massachusetts, who, despite the skepticism of his Republican father, joined "because of Kennedy." Juan Bosch of the Dominican Republic called the Peace Corps "Kennedy in action." A member assigned to Tanganyika came up with a good response for the question "Why did you join?": He remembered the apocryphal story of Emerson's visit to Thoreau while that crusty moralist was in Concord jail. "My dear Thoreau, why are you here?" Thoreau, according to legend, replied, "My dear Emerson, why are you not here?" A 1963 Harris Poll found the Peace Corps to be one of the most popular action of the Kennedy administration. Kennedy's Peace Corps children were, according to Gerard Rice, his "real best and brightest."

Khrushchev, who had earlier sent technical experts to Third World countries, saw the Peace Corps as nothing more than an intensification of the Cold War. Whatever may have been the effectiveness of the Corps itself in its infancy, the goodwill that the Kennedy administration was working so hard to offer and generate was apparently becoming a reality. When the premier threatened Kennedy directly and just 90 miles away from Florida, in the gravest test of the president's ability to act assertively and with restraint, the African nations refused to take the Soviet side. Kennedy regarded this as an important measure of his policy on the troubled continent.

Early in 1962 Castro and the Russians agreed to the secret installation of Soviet missiles on the island even as the Soviets assured the United States that this would never be done. It was the first time the U.S.S.R. had set up offensive missiles outside home borders, as the United States had done years before. And these Cuban missiles were to be closer to the interior of the United States than American installations were to the Soviet Union. The projection was for 42 medium-range (1,100-mile) ballistic missiles, 24 intermediate-range (2,200-mile) missiles, which would never arrive, 48 outdated bombers, and some 22,000 advisers. By October few if any of the sites had yet been armed with nuclear warheads.

Khrushchev's emplacement of missiles could have been another means of neutralizing the Kremlin right, but why did he risk so dangerous a course as possibly placing nuclear missiles in Cuba? Khrushchev's memoirs describe the missiles as an attempt to reestablish the balance of power that Kennedy's swift military buildup had disrupted. The Soviet missile capacity, despite Soviet successes in space, was inferior to that of the United States. The missiles in Cuba might make a contribution, marginal or substantial, to reestablishing a balance of power. But whether distance mattered militarily, in an age when a major war would clutter the skies with missiles from distant continents. is not at all clear. Distance, however, did matter as a gesture of belligerence and as a statement that Cuba was under Soviet protection. Khrushchev later argued in his memoirs that the missiles were palpably defensive: "It would have been preposterous for us to unleash a war against the United States from Cuba. Cuba was 11,000 kilometers from the Soviet Union. Our sea and air communications were so precarious that an attack against the U.S. was unthinkable." He added: "We stationed our armed forces on Cuban soil for one purpose only: to maintain the independence of the Cuban people and to prevent . . . invasion. . . ."

Certainly Cuba itself was frightened by whatever it knew of a series of undercover acts of sabotage labeled Operation MONGOOSE and carried on as the largest single covert program of the CIA. Moreover, rumors of plots to assassinate Castro had attained remarkable credibility. In the 1970s a select Senate committee chaired by Frank Church of Idaho documented eight attempts on Castro's life from 1960 to 1965, some by Cuban refugees. While Robert Kennedy subsequently denied that he or his brother had authorized any plan to murder Castro, they made it clear that they wanted the CIA to bring down the Cuban leader. It is hard to believe that the Kennedys did not mean they wanted Fidel killed, though they later realized this would probably do little to improve the situation in Cuba and might even strengthen Soviet influence. Secretary of Defense McNamara later testified "We were hysterical about Castro at the time of the Bay of Pigs and thereafter, and . . . there was pressure [from both Kennedys] to do something about Castro." Others have reported that an invasion by the United States seemed imminent at one point in the spring of 1962. Perhaps, then, the Cubans and the Soviet Union simply thought of the missiles as a defense against invasion, which would risk tripping the trigger on the whole Soviet nuclear arsenal. But what Khrushchev actually did was to rescue the United States from the moral disadvantage created by the Bay of Pigs.

When air surveillance discovered the nearly completed sites, the administration knew that its response might possibly determine the existence of the Soviet and the American populations. For the mid-October strategy sessions, Kennedy applied what he had learned from the Bay of Pigs as well as from the Berlin crisis. Instead of relying on a single group of advisers, he put together the Executive Committee of the National Security council, ExCom, as it was clickingly termed. Discussion was informal and often in small groups; the idea was to engage in full debate and come up with novel solutions. Soon two alternatives dominated the discussions: an air strike against the missiles and perhaps even the long awaited invasion or a naval quarantine of Cuba.

The debate was not quite between hawks and doves, as the terms were then and thereafter to be employed. The Joint Chiefs, predictably, set their hearts on air strikes, and the Air Force under General Curtis Lemay wanted to strike military targets generally. But Senator Fulbright, for example, also argued in favor of air strikes as defensive measures, less provocative than attacking a Soviet ship that was attempting to run a quarantine in open seas. No one, with the possible exceptions of Adlai Stevenson and Averill Harriman, would have allowed the Soviet Union to complete construction of the missiles. But Robert Kennedy, together with McNamara, argued successfully against a military strike, which Robert, at other times so belligerent, observed would be too much like Pearl Harbor. First Robert stated that he had spoken to the president about the argument, and then he went on to point out that thousands of Cuban and Russian lives would be lost. It took some time for the impact of these points to register with the group, but ultimately they heeded them.

In response to a telegram from Kennedy Khrushchev himself suggested that the United States dismantle some outmoded Jupiter missiles in Turkey in exchange for pulling out of Cuba. Eisenhower had ordered emplacement of the fifteen Jupiters allegedly to bolster NATO, but they had little military value. Some historians have concluded that Kennedy's unwillingness publicly to remove them, on the ground that it would bring the Soviets a propaganda victory, unnecessarily risked nuclear war. But as measured a response as a quarantine on Russian ships was certainly a more sensible act than the gamble of placing the missiles in Cuba in the first place. In a televised address on Monday, October 22, 1962, Kennedy announced the presence of the missiles and informed the public of the quarantine. Distrusting the chief of naval operations (whom he later fired), the president placed McNamara in charge of the operation and provided that every ship enforcing the ban carry Russian-speaking personnel. A harmless tanker was permitted to enter the quarantine area, which had been drawn as close to Cuba as possible. Finally, the first ship carrying equipment usable on the missile bases turned back the following Wednesday, and that Sunday Khrushchev announced that he would dismantle the missiles.

Behind the public events, telegrams shot back and forth across the seas. In one the premier offered to take the missiles away in return for a promise that the United States would not invade Cuba. Events, he said, would join the "knot of war" tighter and tighter if a compromise were not reached. Another telegram asked for the removal of the American missiles from Turkey. This precipitated in ExCom a strong resurgence of demands for an air strike. Then Robert Kennedy proposed that Washington ignore the more bellicose of Khrushchev's two telegrams, publicly avoid the question of the Turkish bases but promise to stay out of Cuba, and privately let him go to the Russians with the word that dismantling the sites on Cuba would bring the withdrawal of the American missiles from Turkey. Bob's legal training was in evidence, for this was what Herbert Parmet calls a "lawyer-like understanding." The attorney general prevailed.

That was how the Cuba missile crisis ended: Khrushchev announced that the Soviet missiles would be withdrawn; President Kennedy told the world that the United States would never invade Cuba and privately canceled Operation MONGOOSE; the missiles were removed from the island, and from Turkey. Critics on the left have said that Kennedy risked nuclear war by forsaking secret diplomacy and speaking openly to the people about the crisis. On the other side, Richard Nixon has said that the president, by not seizing the opportunity to liberate Cuba, "enabled the United States to pull defeat out of the jaws of victory." Since then conservatives have complained that instead of getting rid of Castro, Kennedy guaranteed his safety against invasion, repealed the Monroe Doctrine, and overlooked a Soviet brigade that remained in Cuba for years. The cold warrior mentality is best caught in former Secretary of State Dean Acheson's remark that "so long as we had the thumbscrew on Khrushchev, we should have given it another turn every day." In fact, a United States campaign against Cuba continued, but a more modest one designed to "nourish a spirit of resistance and disaffection."

Debate has continued about using the missile crisis as a guide to foreign policy confrontations. Secretary of Defense Robert McNamara wondered if "there is no such thing as strategy, only crisis management" and, with other civilians, came away with an increased contempt for the military. But without long-term strategic planning, and without a clear sense of military capabilities, the Kennedy administration continued its course into the quagmire of Vietnam. The missile crisis remained a heated issue on its twenty-fifth anniversary, when three analysts concluded in the establishment journal *Foreign Affairs* that "President Kennedy had decided he was not going to initiate war over the missiles in Cuba, but that he would do his utmost to get them removed with the least political cost."

One foreign policy objective of the administration in 1963 grew out of the missile crisis: the relieving tension between the superpowers. The president's pacific speech at American University in June was itself a thaw in the Cold War. He urged that Americans not fall "into the same trap as the Soviets, not to see only a distorted and desperate view of the other side." And later: "We all inhabit this small planet. We all breathe the same air. We all cherish our children's future. And we are all mortal. . . . We must deal with the world as it is and not as it might have been. . . . " The introduction of a hot line between Moscow and Washington for use in emergencies was one more instance of an easing of tensions, an idea that Khrushchev had originally proposed more than a year before. Ten days after the speech at American University the two nations signed an agreement providing for a private teletype, and the hot line was in operation before the end of the summer. "Please explain," came the first reply from the Soviet Union, "what is meant by a quick brown fox jumping over a lazy dog." Averill Harriman also met in 1963 with the Communist Chinese, but a new interpretation by Gorden Chang places the thawing of tensions with the Soviets in the context of Kennedy's fears of China's nuclear arsenal. The final event under Kennedy in easing tensions with the Soviets was an agreement in October 1963 to sell $250 million of wheat to eastern bloc countries.

The strongest of Kennedy's legacies in foreign policy was the atmospheric test ban on nuclear weapons. The ban, widely discussed since the Eisenhower administration, was prompted by the sober mood that followed the missile crisis. After Khrushchev agreed to it in correspondence with the president in May and June 1963, Averill Harriman, the roving ambassador of the Kennedy administration, skillfully and quickly negotiated the Limited Test Ban Treaty, which was initialed in Moscow on August 5. The Senate approved the treaty by a vote of eighty to nineteen in September, despite the opposition of defense contractors, former chiefs of staff Arleigh Burke, Arthur Radford, and Nathan Twining, scientists like Dr. Edward Teller, and the Texas oil billionaire H. L. Hunt, who financed the campaign against it. Taking effect in October, the treaty was a significant event in the forward movement of the Kennedy administration in 1963. Rather than praising Kennedy for moving away from the nuclear retaliation policy of the 1950s, some now condemn him for a power-play attempt to freeze armaments at a time favorable to the United States. But the ban, which ended the dangers of atmospheric fallout, was enormously popular throughout the world. On a trip to the Western states in October Kennedy referred to the end of nuclear fallout and received wild cheers. The trip to these mostly Republican areas took on the character of a campaign swing. While the treaty ended testing in space, in the atmosphere, and under water, Kennedy now realized public support might have enabled him to include an end to all nuclear explosions, hundreds of which continued underground. The enormous costs of the nuclear arms race have continued ever since the Kennedy era when final compromise was a hair's breadth away; the Soviets wanted no more than three on-site inspections as a condition for ending all testing, while the Americans demanded seven.

In the process of ratifying the test ban treaty, the president had skillfully persuaded important Republican conservatives to side with him. These included Republican Senator Everett

Dirksen of Illinois and Congressman Charles Halleck of Indiana, both of whom had favored the quarantine of Cuba over an air strike and after riots in Birmingham had supported a new civil rights bill. The treaty, along with its backing by Dirksen and Halleck, suggested the breadth of the political changes that seemed to be happening: like so much in the Kennedy years, it was symbolically important. It announced, to the unhappiness of the right, that significant contact with the Soviet Union would no longer be defined as an unthinkable breach of American virtue. Many on the right, and some Cold War liberals like Nelson Rockefeller of New York, opposed the treaty. In the years that followed, the debate on foreign policy would take a new form. Right-wingers wanted a continuation of the Cold War that an earlier generation of liberals had crafted; a new left despised it entirely; and liberalism broke apart over Vietnam, its rigid but measured anticommunism at odds with its sense of the complexity and infinite particularity of the world's problems.

V I

Vietnam

As a first-term congressman Jack Kennedy was dimly aware of Indochina, composed of Vietnam, Laos, and Cambodia, from reading *National Geographic* articles that praised France for "modernizing" the peninsular countries. But after visiting Vietnam in 1951, he argued against aiding the French colonialists in Southeast Asia, where they were waging a war against the nationalist leader Ho Chi Minh, who had forged an inseparable blend of nationalism and communism in Vietnam. The Truman administration, however, was already financing about 40 percent of the cost of the hopeless French war. Kennedy spoke of the nationalist hatred in Vietnam of "the white man who bled them, beat them, exploited them, and ruled them." In 1954 Kennedy warned of "an enemy which is everywhere and at the same time nowhere, 'an enemy of the people' which has the sympathy and covert support of the people." These were strong and perceptive criticisms, but Kennedy was by no means alone in making them. Many politicians in both the Truman and Eisenhower years felt much the same way.

In 1957 Kennedy attacked the uncompromising policy of colonialist France in Algeria, seeing there the same pattern of colonial decay that he had witnessed in Vietnam. He spoke frequently of the common "revolutionary tradition" the United States shared with such countries. Once again, though, Kennedy's was by no means a lone voice. And in observing that resistance by the French could damage moderate nationalist Algerians, he was making a conservative argument. He also pointed out the inconsistency of a policy that attacked Soviet hegemony in Hungary and Poland while supporting French colonialism in Vietnam, Algeria, Morocco, and Tunisia. By 1959 Kennedy was keeping quiet about Algeria after receiving sharp criticisms from Democrats ranging from Adlai Stevenson to Dean Acheson. He came to realize how difficult it was for President Charles de Gaulle to accomplish the separation amid political instability and sharp divergence of views within France. Kennedy's stand on Algeria was no doubt sincere; at the same time it presented a good opportunity to assure the Democratic liberals whom he was courting in the late 1950s that he was ready to offer new departures in foreign policy. It was ironic that de Gaulle would later lecture Kennedy in much the same terms that Kennedy had once lectured France about Indochina and Algeria. De Gaulle wrote of Vietnam: "I predict that you will sink step by step into a bottomless military and political quagmire, however much you spend in men and money."

By the time of the French defeat at the battle of Dienbienphu in 1954, Americans were footing 80 percent of the war's cost. Indirectly influencing a peace conference in Geneva, the Eisenhower administration managed to have Vietnam divided along traditional historical boundaries into northern and southern sectors pending a free election in 1956. By then the nationalist, anticommunist leader of the South, Premier Ngo Dinh Diem—resident of the United States for several years before Dienbienphu and shored up by American dollars— was strong enough to hold his territory. But he was not strong enough to win a political contest against Ho Chi Minh, and so refused to hold the promised ballot. President Eisenhower spent millions more in economic and social aid so Diem could fight a mix of nationalist and Communist guerrillas and terrorists, who organized the National Liberation Front in 1960 and become known as the Vietcong. In 1959 at Gettysburg College, Eisenhower urged substantial military aid for Vietnam. Even as Diem's nationalism had enabled the western presence in Vietnam to persist, so the faults of his regime ensured its eventual downfall: a Mandarin temperament that crippled his administrative efforts; the silencing of dissent with arrest and torture; the replacement of elected village chiefs with appointees from Saigon; the use of Catholics to administer Buddhist areas; the forcing of civil servants into the dictator's own political party; widespread corruption; and even an unpopular ban on dancing. Lobbied by Cardinal Spellman who claimed befriending Diem would help Kennedy among conservative Catholics, Kennedy took his side: "This is our offspring—we cannot abandon it, we cannot ignore its needs." A war against communism was different, Kennedy presumed, from a war to protect the colonialists. The example of Ferdinand Marcos in the Philippines was very much on the minds of Americans eager to extend the Cold War into the Third World. Places like Malaya and even the Congo also seemed to demonstrate that insurgency could be stopped. But Vietnam would turn out to be quite different. Changing the enemy from colonialism to communism would not make it easier to win in a xenophobic country long exploited by the West.

Supporting the nationalist Diem not only was the automatic response of a liberal cold warrior of the postwar years but also was in the tradition of Wilsonian internationalism. Americans were their brothers' keepers in a world beset by totalitarians of various hues; and in siding with Diem, Kennedy saw him as a leader at once less oppressive and more promising than his counterpart in the North. Kennedy was right to believe that the country was increasingly under attack by the Communist North, though there were plenty of native opponents of Diem. Vietcong trained in the North were attempting to infiltrate the Buddhist, student, and other antigovernment forces. Kennedy, like Eisenhower, was sold on the domino theory: "I believe it," he said. "China is so large, looms so high just beyond the frontiers, that [South Vietnam's fall] would not only give an improved geographic position for guerrilla assault on Malaya, but . . . also give the impression that the wave of the future in Southeast Asia was China and the Communists." The memory of the fall of China, and the political damage it did to their party, had deeply influenced Democrats. And at that time the promise by Lin Piao of China to wage an extended war against the West was a credible threat to world stability.

At the beginning of the Kennedy involvement in Southeast Asia—a predictable continuation of the Truman and Eisenhower involvements—the administration was chiefly worried about the aggressive rhetoric from the Soviet Union. Just before Kennedy delivered his inaugural address, Khrushchev had reaffirmed his commitment to wars of national liberation, and did so again at the Vienna summit conference a few months later. The Soviets were reacting against the Chinese, who now claimed to be the leaders of the Third World. But instead of seeing Soviet bellicosity as a response to the new Chinese role and instead of looking critically inward after the Bay of Pigs disaster, Robert Kennedy and Maxwell Taylor, soon to be head of the Joint Chiefs of Staff, reiterated their belief that the United States and the Soviets were "locked in a life and death struggle . . . which we may be losing." In analyzing the Bay of Pigs fiasco they argued for the proclamation of a "limited national emergency," which the president refused to issue. But he did heed the recommendation to "review international agreements," which stood in the way of waging the Cold War, and he was willing to ignore the Geneva accords, which placed restrictions on the number of foreign troops in Vietnam.

The president appointed Frederick Nolting, Jr., as ambassador to Vietnam. Nolting believed in Premier Diem's capacities to hold the South, but the Catholic Diem ignored his proposals with Buddhist serenity. A visit to South Vietnam by Vice President Johnson in the spring of 1961, meant to demonstrate continuing United States support for Diem, added to the administration's sense of urgency. Johnson reported a rapidly deteriorating situation: an abortive coup against Diem some months earlier and an increase in Vietcong troop strength from some 4,000 to about 16,000 in a short period. The Vietcong carried American and French weapons, which should have said something about Diem's ARVN forces as well as the lack of Soviet involvement. But since about 1959 the North Vietnamese were supporting the Vietcong in deep violation of the Geneva accords, and Kennedy was impressed by Johnson's alarming and bellicose report. He came to rely on such independent fact-finding missions.

After a visit to Vietnam late in 1961 General Maxwell Taylor and Walt Rostow of the White House staff called for a troop increase there of 8,000 men to make "the United States a limited partner in the war." They recommended that troops be sent as flood control experts to clean up the war-ravaged Mekong Delta, but Kennedy worried that there would be no easy way to retrieve such a force once it had been sent. Kennedy repeatedly vetoed both his advisers' pleas for sending combat troops and for bombing North Vietnam. Diem himself did not want American ground combat troops, which he thought would destroy his appeal in a Vietnam understandably distrustful of foreigners.

Secretary of State Dean Rusk and Secretary of Defense Robert McNamara joined the call for greater involvement. McNamara, though often said to be insensitive to anything unquantifiable and naive about the data provided him by the South Vietnamese, had a better sense of scope than other advisers and recommended a commitment of 200,000 soldiers. But he did not foresee that while the Vietcong were to lose some 290,000 men in the 1960s, the North Vietnamese could and would provide them with 290,000 more. McNamara, who became the administration's point man on Vietnam, liked to talk about making the North Vietnamese bleed and devised various secret hit-and-run attacks against the North. Like

Taylor and Rostow he had an impatient mentality that demanded concrete results; their rashness contrasted with the plodding ways of Eisenhower and his advisers. Acting on the recommendations of his staff, Kennedy approved air strikes in the South that included the dropping of napalm or, in the words of the consumer-minded Pentagon, "Incinderjell," made by Dow Chemical Company, which fastened to human skin and burned. The tactics were scary, but the North Vietnamese were quite willing to die if necessary.

If there was an unconfident voice, it was the president's. After the Bay of Pigs he worried about activist liberal advisers, and so he questioned "the wisdom of involvement in Vietnam since the basis thereof is not completely clear." Korea, he noted, "was a case of clear aggression which was opposed by the United States and other members of the UN. The conflict in Vietnam is more obscure and less flagrant." He contrasted the obscurity of issues in Vietnam to the clarity of positions in Berlin. He would not send combat troops: "They want a force of American troops. They say it's necessary in order to restore confidence and maintain morale. But it will be just like Berlin. The troops will march in; the bands will play; the crowds will cheer; and in four days everyone will have forgotten. Then we will be told we have to send in more troops. It's like taking a drink. The effect wears off, and you have to take another." Such an analogy scotches any idea that he used the war to divert attention at home from growing unrest over civil rights or to stimulate the economy.

Too cautious to send American troops into combat, the president nonetheless allowed soldiers to go to Vietnam in increasing numbers to lead the South Vietnamese into battle, thereby violating the Geneva accords of 1954, which this country had not signed but did consider as normative. The "military advisers" were, according to the president, to "show [the South Vietnamese] how the job should be done—not tell them or do it for them." The restraint was palpable: though as many as 16,000 Americans were in Vietnam by November 1963, just seventy-three were killed. Presidents Johnson and Nixon sent almost a thousand times that number to their deaths. Americans were not doing the fighting, not yet. This phase of the buildup was a necessary but not a sufficient condition for the conflagration of the mid-sixties.

Still it is highly improbable to presume that Kennedy, even though he had not taken the final steps, would ever have pulled out of Vietnam, especially after the neutralization of Laos. Neither Harriman nor George Ball, the advisers who had the most reservations about Vietnam, ever proposed withdrawal. If there was a question open for discourse, it was not "Can we win?" but "Can we win with Premier Diem?" Before Diem was deposed in 1963, the president, some say, had an opportunity to cut his losses and get out. Kennedy evidently believed he had no alternative but to deepen involvement with Saigon. Once the responsibility for Diem's fall was assumed it became an American war.

Using the same argument as the French general who had committed suicide after his country's defeat at Dienbienphu, General Taylor maintained that the Communists would not respond in any substantial way to strong foreign troop involvement. Kennedy felt comfortable with Taylor: a writer of books on strategy and a commandant of West Point at age forty-four as well as head of Lincoln Center for the Performing Arts, he had brains and style, and he looked the part of a general: clean-cut, resolute, distinguished. He taught several languages at West Point and was as familiar with Virgil and Polybius as with Caesar and Clausewitz. He overhauled the Point's curriculum, which had drifted toward a greater emphasis on engineering and the physical sciences. "The cadets should not live in a mental cloister. Their . . . interests must be catholic, avoiding the small horizons sometimes attributed to military men." The new superintendent also deemphasized football, even dropping the annual game with Notre Dame (which was later reinstituted). Taylor was determined to show the Russians that wars of national liberation were not "cheap, safe, and disavowable" but "costly, dangerous, and doomed to failure." The title of the book in which this quotation appears is *The Uncertain Trumpet,* recalling I Corinthians 14:8 "For if the trumpet gives an uncertain sound, who shall prepare himself for battle?" "It is not the purpose of war," he wrote, "to annihilate those who provoked, but to cause them to mend their ways." Rostow talked of "nation-building." These two advisers were particular devotees of counterinsurgent warfare employing South Vietnamese guerrillas, a tactic that appealed to Kennedy even though it was never implemented on a large scale. In a gesture aimed to check the Pentagon, Kennedy made Taylor the Military Representative of the President in July 1961 before promoting him to be chairman of the Joint Chiefs of Staff in 1962.

The president also liked the advice of Brigadier General Edward Lansdale, a legendary figure whose daring and successful exploits against Communist guerrillas in the Philippines impressed him. One story Kennedy enjoyed is that Lansdale, after spreading rumors that a vampire inhabited a disputed area, left a Communist corpse with two holes in his neck and the blood drained from the body. The insurgents fled the area upon finding the bloodless corpse. Lansdale wanted to expand such counterguerrilla "demotic" tactics, designed to capture and solidify the popular will, against the Communists in the land he called the "forest of tigers." It was his idea to defoliate the forests so the Communist guerrillas would have no place to hide, except that he would import Chinese nationalists from Taiwan to cut down the trees—and mow down the Vietcong on the way—rather than to use chemical defoliants. It was Kennedy himself who ordered the use of toxic chemicals, at first called Operation Hades and later Operation Ranch Hand. The goal was to bring large areas within a safe zone of strategic hamlets, either fortified villages or refugee camps surrounded by barbed wire or moats where the rural Vietnamese, herded off their land, would be protected from the Vietcong. The plan was part of a counterguerrilla offensive emphasizing self-defense and civic action, cutting the Vietcong off from the villages and the people. Were it not for objections against the maverick Lansdale from the Departments of State and Defense, he would probably have become ambassador to South Vietnam. General Taylor took a dim view of the harmonica-playing Lansdale: "He could turn out ideas faster than you could pick them up off the floor, but I was never impressed with their feasibility." Lansdale went off to Cuba as part of Operation MONGOOSE to "get rid of" Castro, and the Vietnam war soon turned into a conventional military effort.

Kennedy continued to ponder the domestic political consequences of the loss of French Indochina and at times could sound frankly bellicose. "What I am concerned about is that Americans will get impatient and say that because they don't like events in Southeast Asia or they don't like the government in Saigon . . . we should withdraw. That only makes it easy for the Communists. I think we should stay." He should have remembered the unstable atmosphere in France that grew with the long Algerian war; the United States would suffer a similar instability in the middle and late 1960s. Secretary of State Dean Rusk reports that in the "hundreds" of times he talked with Kennedy about Vietnam, on no single occasion did the president ever whisper any such thing as withdrawal. Former President Eisenhower called the increased presence in Vietnam under Kennedy "absolutely necessary."

Yet a remarkable amount of self-doubt and self-questioning squares with the version of a president trying, as always since the Bay of Pigs, to balance force and caution. In Vietnam he saw analogies to the response he had made to the Soviets in the Cuban missile crisis: in both cases, it seemed to him, outside forces were primarily to blame for the situation. The United States was simply countering the assistance provided by the North Vietnamese, and the Soviets or Chinese, by way of the Ho Chi Minh trail through Laos. When Kennedy made any of his numerous comments about the ambiguities of the Vietnam war—"In the final analysis it is their war," he remarked in September 1963—many liberals could be counted on to chide him for waffling. "No," said *The New York Times*, "it was our war—a war from which we cannot retreat and which we dare not lose."

What Kennedy—this same president who introduced artillery, fighter-bomber aircraft, and American-piloted helicopters into Vietnam—would most have liked was a disengagement on terms that would leave South Vietnam an independent republic. Nine months after his inaugural address, he delivered another speech, quite different in tone, reminding his countrymen "that the United States is neither omniscient nor omnipotent, that we are only 6 percent of the world's population, that we cannot impose our will upon the other 94 percent of mankind, that we cannot right or wrong or reverse each adversity, and that therefore there cannot be an American solution to every world problem." "If the Vietnamese win it, okay, great," Roger Hilsman of State, himself a strong supporter of counterinsurgency, reports the president as saying of the war in the spring of 1963. "But if they don't, we're going to Geneva and do what we did with Laos [set up a neutralist government]." Senator Mike Mansfield has stated that Kennedy wanted a complete military withdrawal from Vietnam after the next presidential election. In October he asked McNamara, the chief optimist in his prediction that the war would be over in 1965, to tell the press that 1,000 troops were coming home, that American aid was promised only "at this time," and that by the end of 1965 all American troops would be pulled out. "And tell them that means the helicopter pilots too," the president shouted as McNamara went to meet reporters. Kennedy told his defense secretary that he would "close out" the Vietnam war in 1965 "whether it was in good shape or bad." The Pentagon Papers contain much the same Kennedy plan for withdrawal. He thought seriously of sending John Kenneth Galbraith, his ambassador to India, on a mission to Hanoi, but Rusk, fearing it might undermine Diem, vetoed that suggestion. Only three days before he was killed, Kennedy sent an aide, Michael Forrestal, to Cambodia and told him that when he returned he was to "organize an in-depth study of every possible option we've got in Vietnam, including how to get out of there. We have to review this whole thing from the bottom to the top." The president went on to reveal to Forrestal his own doubts about the commitment to South Vietnam that he had inherited from Eisenhower, and Eisenhower from Truman.

Toward the end of his life Kennedy was evidently groping, steadfastly refusing either to accept an irrevocable loss of South Vietnam or to make a heavy irreversible involvement for that country's rescue. Robert Kennedy gave his answer to whether the United States would have sent combat troops if a South Vietnamese defeat seemed likely: "Well, we'd have faced that when we came to it."

Kennedy's one minimally successful act in Indochina during his presidency was to communicate directly with Khrushchev about Laos, which lay west of Vietnam. Here the president went in another direction from the pull of some experts who wanted greater explicit involvement in that part of the world. His adviser Walt Rostow, true to form, was anxious to send troops to the "land of the thousand elephants," but the terrain of the landlocked country made it virtually indefensible. Kennedy leaned more toward Averell Harriman's advice to neutralize Laos but to support counterguerrilla activities against the increasing influence of North Vietnam. In Laos the United States had been supporting a rightist faction and the Soviets a Communist faction. At one point in May 1962 Kennedy sent the Seventh Fleet to the nearby Gulf of Siam and mobilized thousands of American troops along the Laotian border; these actions had the dual aims of inhibiting the Communists and forcing right-wing leaders into a coalition. In July 1962 fourteen nations agreed on a neutralist government under Prince Souvanna Phouma and agreed also on a relatively simple disengagement implemented later under a tripartite commission of neutralists, Communists, and anticommunists. Kennedy's support of a neutralist Laos was a departure from the thinking of the Eisenhower years, which had considered neutralism immoral. Eisenhower said that trying to establish a successful coalition government in Laos was "the way we lost China." Neither the North Vietnamese nor allied forces lived up to the agreements, and by 1964 neutralization had failed just as the entire American policy in Indochina was failing.

In 1963 Harriman reported from Vietnam almost exactly what the Vietcong were reporting to the North: Diem could not last as long as his regime continued to be "repressive, dictatorial, and unpopular." But during the Laotian debates Attorney General Robert Kennedy had asked somewhat portentously: "What would be the best place to stand and fight in Southeast Asia?" Vietnam was the answer—not Laos, where the North Vietnamese would repeatedly break the peace.

The battle of Ap Bac in the Mekong Delta in January 1963 demonstrated to Kennedy that the modest improvements in South Vietnam of 1962 were only temporary. There, only fifty miles from Saigon, ARVN forces surrounded a Vietcong battalion a quarter the size of their own forces. American planes, helicopters, and artillery backed up Diem's forces; but the overly cautious South Vietnamese, having taken sixty-one casualties, three of whom were Americans, obligingly opened an escape route to let the tough resisters break through to freedom. An American general called the battle a victory for Saigon because "we took the objective"—a piece of contested territory the enemy had abandoned more than a day before. The month previous, Senator Mike Mansfield and three other senators, after a visit to Vietnam, warned that the struggle was becoming an "American war" little improved since

1955. General Taylor recognized the problem retrospectively in 1984: "Before we ally ourselves to another country, we must ascertain to what extent they can exploit our help. We know the great effort we expended on Vietnam. The large percentage of the effort was unusable." He also recalled: "You should never let television on the battlefield." Instead of looking for a way out, the Kennedy administration took a dangerous course: it sought a change of government from Diem. Increasingly corrupt and at odds with the anti-Catholic Buddhist majority almost as much as with the Communists, Diem's regime also suffered from his practice of promoting within the military on the basis of personal loyalty rather than ability. Seeking to make his policy bipartisan, Kennedy appointed Henry Cabot Lodge, Jr., who had been his liberal Republican opponent in his 1952 senatorial campaign, as the new American ambassador. Then with the encouragement of Harriman, fresh from the signing of the nuclear test-ban treaty in Moscow, the administration implicitly urged the South Vietnamese military to stage a coup against Diem. Harriman obtained the president's permission for this desperate approach. Deaf but not blind, the seventy-one-year old son of a railroad tycoon saw that Diem was out of touch with his people. Harriman also disliked the strong role the Department of Defense was playing in the war, particularly its use of napalm and defoliants, and he wanted a more important role for the State Department. Most of all, he wanted a lesser role for the United States.

With support neither from the army nor from the non-Catholic elements in the South, Diem was cursed also by his sister-in-law, Madame Ngo Dinh Nhu, who had great influence on the premier; she was dominant in his household. In June 1963 when Thich Quang Duc, a seventy-three-year-old Buddhist monk, doused himself with gasoline and set himself on fire, she called the Buddhists "communist dupes" and "clapped gaily" at the news. Both photojournalists and television crews transmitted pictures of Duc's face, silent but contorted in agony, and his charred body collapsed on the street. "All they have done is barbecue a bonze [Buddhist priest]," said Madame Nhu on hearing of another such incident. These events alarmed Kennedy, who instantly recalled the impact of television's recent portrayal of the Birmingham riots. "How could this have happened? Who are these people? Why didn't we know about them before?" he demanded. Diem would not repudiate his sister-in-law but declared: "My policy of reconciliation with the Buddhists is irreversible." Diem's brother explained that the monk had drugged himself. With increasing power over Diem in the last two years, Ngo Dinh Nhu had a record of anti-Americanism and was even carrying on negotiations with the North Vietnamese. He and his wife prevailed on the premier to launch a series of attacks against Buddhist pagodas in major cities. Diem's praetorian guard fired into Buddhist crowds, killing women and children, and arrested 1,400 monks and nuns. Similar acts of repression were directed against rioting students. The violence and martial law stunned Washington and radicalized the Buddhist leadership. Kennedy's patience was exhausted. As for overthrowing Diem, he said that the "Vietnamese are doing that for themselves and don't need any outside help." The alternatives to Diem included General Duong Van Minh, known as "Big Minh" because of his imposing height and bulk. Minh had long urged that the United States exercise control over Diem's autocratic methods.

A telegram drafted by Harriman and others and signed by the president gave Lodge astonishing carte blanche both on how to accomplish a coup, which had been suggested to the ambassador by the South Vietnamese military, and on replacing Diem. "We shall back you to the hilt," the message said. Lodge agreed on the need for a coup: "There is no possibility, in my view, that the war can be won under a Diem administration." The plan, however, took a couple of months to implement. Kennedy was frustrated: on September 2, 1963, he candidly admitted to CBS News, "I don't think that unless a greater effort is made by the government to win popular support . . . the war can be won out there." Later in the interview he added with customary indecision, "We . . . made this effort to defend Europe. Now Europe is quite secure. We also have to participate—we may not like it—in the defense of Asia." As late as the speech he planned to deliver at the Trade Mart in Dallas on the afternoon of November 22, Kennedy had written "Our assistance to these nations can be painful, risky and costly, as is true in Southeast Asia today. But we dare not weary of the test." In that talk he cast the United States as the "Watchman of the World."

The generals were understandably cautious, and the Kennedy administration, never more deeply divided, vacillated. Everyone feared Madame Nhu, dubbed the "Dragon Lady" by the foreign press. By now she was over the edge. She had a third particularly brutal brother draw up a hit list of Americans to be assassinated. She believed Ambassador Lodge was planning to have her murdered. She had a monument that was dedicated to two national heroines carved in her own likeness. She orchestrated plans to kill the "miraculous fish," a giant carp famous in a northern province as a "disciple of Buddha." Soldiers sprayed its pond with automatic weapons and then mined the waters to kill the carp but were unsuccessful. Finally they lured it to the surface with bread and tossed hand grenades at it, killing everything in the pond except the giant fish. The fish's indestructibility persuaded pilgrims to carry away holy water from the pond, and even South Vietnamese soldiers filled their canteens. Madame Nhu planned to poison the pond after her return from a trip to the United States—where she referred to American officers as "little soldiers of fortune."

The story of the fish appalled Robert Kennedy, who took a greater role in the Vietnam debates after sharp division within the administration over the Harriman telegram. "We have to be tough" with Diem, Robert said. General Victor Krulak, an interested party with a stake in counterinsurgency training, made a brief visit on yet another fact-finding mission and declared that the war was going well; but the civilian emissary, Joseph Mendenhall of the State Department, reported that it was doing badly and warned of a religious war, calling the major cities "cities of hate . . . living under [a] reign of terror." On hearing their reports, the president asked, "Did you two gentlemen visit the same country?" He sent McNamara and his assistant William Bundy on a ten-day trip that confirmed Diem's unpopularity.

The generals led by Big Minh finally struck on November 1, 1963. When the premier supposedly at his palace refused to surrender despite a lack of support troops, a Catholic colonel was drafted by the Buddhist generals to lead an assault. Diem had in fact safely fled to the home of a Chinese businessman, maintaining phone contact with the palace switchboard. Americans were asked to fly the notorious Diem brothers out of the country, but no long-range aircraft could be provided for twenty-four hours. After it became apparent that the two Diem brothers had been assassinated, the generals explained that the Diems had committed suicide—or rather, "accidental suicide," when it was pointed out that it was unlikely that two Roman Catholics would take their own lives. On hearing of their fate, Maxwell Taylor has written, "Kennedy leaped to his feet and rushed from the room with such a look of shock and dismay on his face which I had never seen before." "It shook him personally," reports Michael Forrestal, "bothered him as a moral and religious matter." Perhaps the president never ordered any assassinations, including Castro's, but allowed the CIA to act there with its own Byzantine indirection.

Many liberals, like the journalist David Halberstam, *The New York Times* correspondent in Saigon whom the president had unsuccessfully tried to get transferred, welcomed the deposing of Diem. Halberstam's later book, *The Best and the Brightest,* is the story of how the liberals escalated the war. The radical columnist I. F. Stone wrote: "How many of us—on the left now—did not welcome the assassination of Diem and his brother Nhu in South Vietnam? We all reach for the dagger, or the gun, in our thinking when it suits our political view to do so."

If the removal of Diem brought the United States further trouble, his staying in office might have resulted in something worse—civil war. Diem had lost what some Asian cultures call "the mandate of heaven," the support of his people. Robert Kennedy wondered whether the assassination might provide an opportunity for withdrawal. But after the murder of the Diem brothers (the even more brutal third brother was dispatched a few days later, and another, the archbishop of Hue, escaped along with Madame Nhu by virtue of being out of the country) a deterioration of the military position, long cloaked by the old administration, became obvious. The coup was followed by eighteen months of revolving-door governments, greater instability in the provinces where local leaders were replaced, and more open support of the insurgents by the North Vietnamese military. In response, 216,000 American servicemen would go to Vietnam, and 53,000 would never return. Deposing Diem led not to a stronger government in South Vietnam but to a greater sense of American obligation there. The client state had caught its prey, but now there was no Diem between the United States and the chaos. The events showed the difficulty of trying to moderate the Saigon government without weakening it, to increase American influence in Vietnam without making Saigon look like a puppet. The fortunes of the war reflected this difficulty: watchfulness in 1961, optimism in 1962, growing alarm in 1963.

Kennedy was assuredly trapped by the incremental policy that Truman and Eisenhower had followed. But in Kennedy's years the American presence had grown to a size at which its character could not be easily limited. The president's encouragement toward the removal of Diem suggests that he was less prepared than some other presidents had been to tolerate oppressive governments whose only credentials were that they were rigidly anticommunist. Kennedy also understood better than had Americans in the 1950s the role of neutralism in the world, which Eisenhower's Secretary of State John Foster Dulles had equated with opportunism if not outright alliance with the Soviets. Yet through ignorance or consent Kennedy allowed the CIA to try to subvert the Cambodian leader Prince Norodom Sihanouk, who drew on popular loyalties and stood for a hope of a peaceful Cambodia. What Kennedy only dimly sensed was the diversities of causes and of kinds of revolution. While the world was still divided into Communist and anticommunist blocs, it was also a patchwork of Cambodias, Vietnams, and Indonesias, where revolutionary conditions were of the home-grown variety.

Would Kennedy have crossed the covert action threshold in Vietnam as Lyndon Johnson eventually did? Would he have committed more and more ground troops and bombed North Vietnam? What can be made of this president whose public and private statements were at cross purposes, a man who seemed to want to put troops in and bring troops home? Certainly Kennedy was afraid that our reputation for guaranteeing another country's peace would be jeopardized if we withdrew; certainly he saw the Sino-Soviet split as liberating an unrestrained, hostile, nuclear China that had to be taught the lessons of international stability; certainly the thrust of his whole administration was to pursue the Cold War in the Third World. Almost certainly he would have escalated the war; it is likely that other scenarios are wishful thinking on the part of his admirers. But his encouragement of the coup against Diem suggests that his administration was less prepared than others to ignore the character of governments that were strongly anticommunist but at the same time nondemocratic. Kennedy's meddling in Vietnam was probably one of the least insensitive meddlings of Americans abroad. In his hesitations about troop increases, as in his rejection of hardline advice in the Cuban missile and Berlin Wall crises, Kennedy appeared more cautious and aware than most of his circle of advisers. It is ironic that most Americans remember that their country somehow went downhill after Kennedy's death, yet the down escalator was the Vietnam War in which he played a principal role. Withdrawing from Vietnam would have taken the kind of political courage this pragmatic president so much admired yet so rarely demonstrated. But what he apparently looked for more than courage was prudent judgment. The debate over what would have been prudent judgment in Vietnam will long continue.

VII

Fires of Frustration

"No STATESMAN," Abraham Lincoln wrote in the mid-1850s as the Civil War approached, "can safely disregard" the moral aversion people increasingly felt toward slavery. That, argues Richard Hofstadter in a famous essay on the Great Emancipator, was the "key to Lincoln's growing radicalism. As a practical politician he was naturally very much concerned with those public sentiments no statesman can safely disregard." A similar compounding of political and moral sensibilities moved John Kennedy to speak for the first time with unmistakable moral anger about racial injustice in 1963: "No city or state or legislative body can prudently choose to ignore . . . the fires of frustration and discord . . . burning in every city."

The civil rights movement had been stirring for years. Foreshadowed in government appeals for national unity during World War II and then in President Harry Truman's desegregation of the armed services and his establishment of a comprehensive study of social discrimination, the civil rights movement gained a major impetus in the Supreme Court decision of 1954, *Brown v. Board of Education of Topeka, Kansas.* The case repealed the longstanding criterion of "separate but equal" under which public schools had been allowed to practice segregation. In 1955 when Rosa Parks refused to move from her seat on a bus in Montgomery, Alabama, and the black community there waged a successful boycott of the city's buses, an invisible line had been crossed. In 1957 President Dwight Eisenhower sent federal troops to force the court-ordered desegregation of Central High School in Little Rock, Arkansas. By so doing he probably lost the South for the Republican Party in 1960. During the winter just preceding Kennedy's election, black and white students in defiance of segregation ordinances sat down and drank coffee together at Southern lunch counters, first in Greensboro, North Carolina, and then within a few weeks throughout much of the South. In the summer of the next year, white racists assaulted freedom riders on their journey by bus to desegregate Southern transportation routes, a journey revolutionary not only in its rejection of racial customs but in its nonviolent resistance new to the staid conventions of twentieth-century American politics. In the fall of 1962 Mississippi's governor Ross Barnett fulminated against the enrollment of the first black student, James Meredith, at Ole Miss, where mobs took over the principal state campus and killed two men. In Birmingham the following spring Alabama's chief policeman, Bull Conner, turned police dogs and fire hoses on blacks; and then that September Klansmen dynamited four black children to death in the basement of a Baptist Church while they were singing a hymn in Sunday school class.

The civil rights movement bespoke a nearly miraculous liberation of minds and institutions from racial conventions seemingly set in iron. This movement for sudden freedom, which desegregated a bus or a train in an instant, had little in common with a president who appeared completely opportunistic and utilitarian on the race issue, a politician who twice voted to weaken civil rights bills in the 1950s and who spent more than two years in the White House before proposing any civil rights legislation. In his vice-presidential and presidential bids Kennedy relied for support on the South's most outspokenly segregationist governors, and he omitted civil rights from a list of the "real issues of 1960." Partly the conjunction of Kennedy and civil rights was a matter of coming to the presidency at the right moment. The civil rights movement had been stirring since the Montgomery bus boycott late in 1955 and the forced integration of Little Rock's Central High School in 1957. By the time of the Kennedy administration the movement was on the brink of a moral reformation. When Kennedy spoke his strong words about racial injustice in 1963, his presidency, now an active if nervous partner in the movement, gained thereby a moral high ground it had not anticipated. That transformation was not entirely accidental.

Kennedy's trust went to technology and experts, forces that would seem far distant in spirit from those of the civil rights rebellion. But new technological forces had great power in the 1960s. Television, for example, which greatly affected the course of the civil rights movement, enabled Kennedy to present himself less as a politician and more as an independent force for moral reformation. Television allowed the Kennedy family to enter the homes of all the nation's other families, a bit toney, perhaps, but gracious guests nonetheless. Television in good part rendered the major events of the early sixties into public phenomena significant not only in their purpose and their results but in the fact of being phenomena. The police dogs and fire hoses at Birmingham were such collective events, and seeing them in turn set the president angrily against the racists. The picture of a police dog attacking a black woman made him "sick," he told reporters. The Kennedy inaugural address, with its calls to growth and combat, had itself been a public event. James Meredith said that speech had spurred him to apply to the University of Mississippi the very next day and some freedom riders remembered that stirring speech with its elevated rhetoric as spurring their dangerous treks. Yet the address said nothing beyond a general call for "human rights at home and around the world"; and during the presidential campaign the religious controversy had overshadowed the race issue. But in the early sixties the media portrayed the civil rights movement as the major news event that it deserved to be.

The inaugural was but the first occasion in a collective

stream of experience that the nation associates with the Kennedy presidency. "His actual, tangible impact on history," Louise FitzSimons observes in the course of her severe commentary on Kennedy's foreign policy, "was not significant enough to explain his enormous psychological impact, the indefinable way in which John F. Kennedy touched people throughout the world." Why was it that in villages of India photographs of Ghandi, Nehru, and Kennedy hung side by side? Kennedy's death also won him a place in the memory of his own nation, as the central public figure in a confident time. This memorable quality that Kennedy conveyed was felt particularly by black Americans. One black woman would later remember "Like a good book the life of John F. Kennedy steals inside and has somehow made me different. . . . Everyone I know loved him with a sort of possessiveness." The adulation of most blacks for Kennedy angers many serious American leftists. For what had this president done to deserve such love, so cautious in his recognition of a movement that, in retrospect, appears to constitute the visible and inescapable moral imperative of his presidential years?

On his own initiative, he did nothing striking. But his administration came at a time when political issues offered more of the hope and less of the distress that was to characterize issues thereafter, when the country seemed poised, in its science and technology as well as its social arrangements, at the edge of some futuristic transformation. The witness of the civil rights demonstrations, rooted in Southern evangelical churches, and the cold efficient promise of the space program demarcated polar opposites in American culture, but together they gave energy to the moment of Kennedy's administration. His presidency had a style consonant with that moment, and perhaps it had also the shrewdness along with the conscience to connect with it by some appropriate political gestures. The Kennedy style made government service and public commitment particularly appealing to young people, who became increasingly active in the civil rights movement, the Peace Corps, and public debates of many kinds. Many more young people wrote letters to this president than to any other president. "The biggest single influence that helped the formation of SDS [Students for a Democratic Society]," recalls Robert Greenblatt, an early member, "was John F. Kennedy."

For blacks the new freedom had the press of a nation's history behind it. The Civil War did not eliminate slavery or degradation, and blacks were subjected to decades of massive oppression; after the "Jim Crow" segregation laws of the 1890s it almost seemed as though the South was the winner of that war. However, the civil rights movement reversed the nation's course and gave a new vitality to morally aware Americans. For a growing number of people this new freedom brought a sense that life could be immediately more promising, that America had not forgotten its idealistic heritage.

When Kennedy took office, he found the economy ready for stimulus, public schools in need of reform, and the Supreme Court ready to implement a major change in Southern custom—in the face of billboards that sprang up across the South after 1954 calling for Chief Justice Earl Warren's impeachment. In the next decade many victories came to progressive Americans who brought some optimism to national problems: the civil rights acts and poverty programs; massive federal funds spent on education, housing, and hospital care; tax cuts that generated larger revenues; and American astronauts who reached the moon. The legislative work of a generation was accomplished in about three years under a Kennedy-Johnson coalition founded on the symbolic memory of John Kennedy.

But the last Congress of the Eisenhower years, though Democratic by 280 to 155 in the House and by 66 to 34 in the Senate, had defeated a Medicare bill sponsored by Kennedy and also rejected a public housing law, minimum wage legislation, and aid to schools. The Democratic platform of 1960, drafted by the liberal Chester Bowles, promised action on civil rights, including power for the attorney general to seek court injunctions to enforce existing laws. Then in a short congressional session after the conventions, liberal Democrats joined conservative Southerners to table a civil rights bill that Republicans had introduced to embarrass Kennedy. In response he and other senators promised to offer a bill in the first postelection session to "implement the pledge of the Democratic platform." The candidate even added a separate statement: "In order to implement this pledge and assure prompt action, I have asked Senator [Joseph] Clark and Representative [Emanuel] Celler to constitute a committee to prepare a comprehensive civil rights bill, embodying our platform commitments, for introduction at the beginning of the next session." The president in fact never proposed new laws until 1963. When Celler introduced a bill in the House in 1961, the White House press secretary pointedly backed away from giving it official support. Perhaps Kennedy would have lost Southern votes on other social legislation had he pushed a civil rights bill before it was certain to pass. Indeed social funding bills lost votes in he South after Kennedy supported a new civil rights law in 1963: congressmen even voted against funding that would benefit their own districts. His defenders explain that the narrowness of his election victory and of his party's margin in Congress gave him second thoughts. About 40 percent of the 261 Democrats in the new House were conservative Southerners. "The reason," Ted Sorensen wrote apologetically for not pushing liberal bills such as civil rights, "was arithmetic." In the presidential campaign itself, moreover, Kennedy had increasingly made promises to take direct executive action on civil rights. The trouble is that he delayed for eighteen months on the most symbolically and practically important of his campaign promises: to outlaw segregation in federally supported housing.

Kennedy himself, drawn to adventure stories, to James Bond novels, and elite military exploits, was —at least when he had the patience for it—also drawn to the slow arts of political compromise. Even if he entered the presidency as a liberal, he was apparently comfortable with a national legislature that could not be hurried into progressive laws. Nor did his background promise an assault on racial discrimination. *Profiles in Courage* purveys the stereotype of Reconstruction as a military occupation imposed on the war-ravaged South. No president before John Kennedy, Abraham Lincoln included, could meet more than the smallest test for racial justice, or for open discussion of the issue, on the terms later largely accepted. But no president had been put to the test by any movement as highly visible and moral as the civil rights forces of the sixties. They demanded absolute and uncompromised equality, an end to private and public discrimination, to stereotypes, to the range of nightmares and cruelties that have attended racism in this country. Indisputably, the Kennedy administration was alien at its roots from the work of protesters in the South and especially the courageous civil rights workers in the Southern back country. Neither rejection of his Irish ancestors by Boston Brahmins nor the recurring story that he had been rejected at Groton Preparatory School for being Irish seems to have much bothered John Kennedy.

Certainly an optimistic liberalism was foreign to his character. "There is always some inequality in life," he mused at a press conference in Greenfield, Massachusetts, on March 21, 1962. "Some men are killed in war, and some are wounded, and some men never leave the country, and some men are stationed in the Antarctic and some men are stationed in San Francisco. It is very hard in military or personal life to assure complete equality." A detached skepticism could inform, indeed toughen, a commitment to civil rights, which means a commitment to resist the downward drag of human nature and the appetites of the mob. But it is not in the typical style of twentieth-century liberalism.

Kennedy's first presidential actions did not suggest militancy on the issue. After the election and before he took of-

fice, he appointed a task force to study just about every problem except that of discrimination. He was more conscious of
how America's treatment of blacks looked in the third world
than he was of the moral questions at home. But he was conscious enough of the problem to appoint forty-one blacks to
important posts within two months. Kennedy must have
thought the chances of new legislation hopeless for the moment, inasmuch as he could not even get the appointment of
the black economist, Robert C. Weaver, to be Secretary of Urban Affairs with cabinet rank. The civil rights movement perceived the administration as cautious and unfriendly; yet by
1963 its activity through the Justice Department made it the
most hated federal administration in the deep South for a
century.

The president did not choose for assistant attorney general
for civil rights the dedicated Harris Wofford, who had proposed his telephoning Coretta King during the campaign
when her husband, Martin Luther King, was imprisoned because of his civil rights work in the South. Instead he acted
on the advice of his old professional football player friend
Byron White, who was a conservative Rhodes scholar from
Yale and Washington, a corporate lawyer, later a Kennedy ap-
pointee to the Supreme Court, and one of this century's most
conservative members of the Court. At White's recommendation Kennedy selected Burke Marshall, also of Yale Law
School.

Marshall captured the Kennedy administration's approach
to civil rights. A patient negotiator, he had been a member of
the American Civil Liberties Union and had early argued for
the use of federal registrars to enroll Southern black voters.
Few were registered under the Voter Education Project that
the administration backed. Yet the effort brought money into
the hands of the movement, awakening some black activism
and giving it organizational structure. But voter registration
was hardly safe work for young civil rights workers: rural

Georgia, let alone Mississippi and Alabama, could hold a grim fate for them. Like Kennedy himself, who treated Southern congressmen with a degree of deference, Marshall disliked the use of federal power to coerce civil rights, much preferring the mode of compromise and agreement. He opposed the Civil Rights Commission's plan to hold hearings in Mississippi to publicize conditions there, and he objected as well to the Commission's wish to withhold federal funds from offending states. He labeled as "essentially negative and punitive" the withholding of funds from segregated school districts. He recoiled from any efforts to integrate housing nationwide ("a pretty drastic step legally and constitutionally"), and in 1964 at Columbia University he argued that the central government's police power could not deal effectively with the complex race problem without destroying the federal system. For decades legal conservatives, or legal realists as they are sometimes called, had similarly refrained from using the government to challenge unjust social institutions, and so the injustices continued. As late as the mid-1980s at a forum on Long Island, Marshall was to argue that the introduction of civil rights legislation in 1961 and 1962 had been useless "political posturing" and a waste of congressional time since a filibuster could have killed it.

One black woman has remembered of the early sixties that "when you had JFK, you had two Presidents—JFK and RFK." Attorney General Robert Kennedy was by turns passionate and prudent. Like his father he delighted in using whatever power he could lay his hands on, against radicals in the McCarthy era or against labor racketeers, about whom he published a book, *The Enemy Within*. But later, against an enemy within that was more deeply defiant of American justice, he made only selective use of the weapons of the federal government; the reason civil rights took so much of his time was mainly that it was so explosive an issue. Robert brought a few black attorneys into the Justice Department, along with Ramsey Clark, John Seigenthaler, John Doar, and Archibald Cox.

He made a strong early speech at the University of Georgia in May 1961 praising two newly integrated black students as freedom fighters. No other attorney general had spoken on civil rights in the South in the twentieth century. One of the students, Charlayne Hunter, much later became a nationally prominent television newscaster. The speech announced RFK's determination to work for racial justice. Yet he did not endorse the Democratic party's strong campaign platform on civil rights, and he feared the example of Eisenhower's employment of federal troops at Little Rock.

Beginning that spring James Farmer's Congress of Racial Equality sent its courageous members on freedom rides through the South in buses, defying state and local statutes requiring segregation of bus terminals. Farmer even sent an itinerary of the rides to Kennedy, the FBI, and the Greyhound and Trailways Bus Lines but got no response. "Emotionally, I am totally in sympathy with them," Robert Kennedy said, but he feared that the testing would force federal intervention. Still, he did act to protect the riders, if not to give countenance to their journey. When a freedom bus was firebombed in Anniston, Alabama, and its occupants roughed up by Klansmen, he ordered J. Edgar Hoover's FBI to investigate, resulting in four arrests within a week. When the riders arrived in Birmingham, Robert Kennedy's administrative assistant, Seigenthaler, flew south to watch over them and successive groups, providing whatever defense against mob violence the Justice Department could furnish.

New riders, coming along the same route, had been promised protection by Alabama Governor John Patterson. Though a distinguished opponent of political corruption and a racial moderate by Southern standards at the time, Patterson decided against giving adequate protection to the riders and by his remarks incited that state's rednecks. Freedom riders proceeded from Birmingham to Montgomery, where the local police, stationed just two blocks away, did not appear at the terminal to protect them as promised by the state. Seigenthaler, who had accompanied the freedom riders, was hit on the head with an iron pipe while trying to rescue a black woman demonstrator, and lay unconscious on the ground for almost half an hour. To Robert Kennedy's later disgust the FBI men on the scene only took notes.

At this point the federal government acted briefly with real initiative. The president deputized immigration agents and prison guards as federal marshals under Byron White. That night the marshals protected the Reverend Martin Luther King, Jr., at a local church, which was surrounded by a mob. Finally Governor Patterson called up the National Guard to restore order. White, who believed that blacks needed money more than they needed civil rights, announced that marshals would not intervene if police arrested the freedom riders: the Justice Department, in its obvious discomfort over the whole business of the rides, apparently looked on police detention as a form of custodial care. On White's invitation, the state police arrested the riders when they tried to desegregate the bus terminal in Jackson, the capital. Since all this activity was very procedural, White was satisfied that justice and the safety of the riders were being served. A true conservative, he observed that they would get adequate counsel. Segregationist federal judges refused to dismiss the arrests, which the Supreme Court later reversed in 1965. Both Kennedys desperately wanted to defuse the situation, and even Martin Luther King agreed to a moment's pause—a "lull" as he termed it.

The demonstrations, and more arrests, resumed later in the summer. In September 1961, the Interstate Commerce Commission began enforcing the Supreme Court mandate of desegregation in interstate transportation terminals, which Robert Kennedy had asked for as early as May. Some areas, however, refused to obey. In Albany, Georgia, 700 blacks were arrested that December, among them Reverend King. Burke Marshall obtained the release of the prisoners and an agreement to desegregate public transportation facilities. But the city reneged and the problem continued to fester. The community wide black movement in Albany would be copied else-where, notably in Birmingham in 1963.

The administration never pushed the South hard; the Ken-nedys thought calls for immediate freedom were irresponsi-ble and no more likely of realization than the cries for segre-gation forever. Finding not a single black district court judge in the United States, Kennedy did appoint a few, but segre-gationist judges continued to reach the bench in the South in accord with the tradition of approval from the states' senators for such appointments. Had Kennedy challenged the custom, the Senate Judiciary Committee, then headed by James East-land of Mississippi, would probably never have cleared the appointment of Thurgood Marshall—who argued the Brown case in 1954 and who would later be appointed to the Su-preme Court—and four other blacks to the federal courts. In addition, the administration got eight integrationists onto the famous Fifth Circuit that included the deep South. And in extenuation of the appointment of William A. Cox, who spoke of "niggers" and "chimpanzees" in open court, it should be observed both that the American Bar Association had given him its best ("Extremely Well Qualified") rating and that before his appointment he had promised the attorney general that he would enforce the law of the land.

The contradiction between a segregationist judiciary and a voter registration program dependent on the courts for its enforcement only slowly dawned on Marshall and Robert Kennedy. No government contracts were canceled because of job discrimination: the administration ran away from that idea as if it were a rattlesnake, said a member of the Civil Rights Commission. John Kennedy had criticized Eisenhower for tolerating segregation in federally funded housing, but it took him almost two years before he eliminated it by executive order. He was about to sign the order eight months after tak-ing office but held back for fear of jeopardizing Robert Weav-er's appointment to the cabinet; when he did sign, the scope was narrowed, because the administration knew how explosive an issue housing was throughout the country. Quite a few Northern liberal Democrats from suburban districts even urged Kennedy to delay the order until after the midterm elections, which he did.

The Kennedy record on civil rights has bright moments, and its tone was superior to that of the Eisenhower years— though President Eisenhower's military enforcement of school desegregation in Little Rock, in contravention of the will of the governor of Arkansas, was of incalculable importance as a break with a longstanding federal practice of allowing the South to defy the Constitution.

As early as his inauguration day the president telephoned a cabinet secretary to ask why there had been no blacks in the Coast Guard marching band and was astonished to find that no blacks were enrolled in the entire Coast Guard Academy; vigorous recruiting efforts began forthwith. At Kennedy's insistence a policy of minority recruiting spread to all government agencies. In May 1961, before the freedom rides, Robert Kennedy wrote to forty-five law school deans asking for names of black lawyers and black law students the Justice Department might recruit. In a notable innovation, Marshall sent lawyers into the South to investigate violations of voting rights and permitted them to initiate remedial actions. No doubt this approach was eminently conservative, since it was only defending a constitutional right. But even so cautious a step as this inflamed Alabama and Mississippi. The administration persuaded Maryland to pass a public accommodations law and persuaded its governor to apologize to black diplomats turned away from a restaurant in that state while traveling from New York to the capital. In Washington, D.C., the president appointed the first black district commissioner.

Robert Kennedy asked Congress to forbid literacy tests for voting and instead use a sixth-grade education as the criterion. That a bill to this effect failed to pass no doubt indicated the fate a general civil rights bill would have met. But at the president's request and through a carefully crafted plan, Congress sent to the states for later passage the Twenty-fourth Amendment outlawing the poll tax. The government told universities that federal funds might be withheld if there was evidence of discrimination. Through the appointment in March 1961 of another President's Committee on Equal Employment Opportunity chaired by Vice President Johnson, the administration won some agreements from businesses to improve their minority hiring practices. But at least until 1963 the group relied too heavily on voluntary compliance and accomplished little. Johnson recommended that the civil rights bill of 1963 await passage of the tax reform bill, but he also advised the president to cast his message for rights in such a way that "it almost make[s] a bigot out of nearly anybody that's against him." Johnson himself made a strong speech at Gettysburg that May arguing for civil rights—and speaking in a Southern accent. Activists were appointed to the Civil Rights Commission, most notably the deans of Harvard and Howard law schools. The White House press pool and its photographers' association were at last desegregated. The president withdrew his application to the District's Cosmos Club when membership was denied a prominent black. And, unlike Eisenhower, Kennedy regularly entertained blacks in the White House, as did Robert Kennedy in his Virginia home. The president insisted that the Civil Service Commission establish minority recruitment visits to colleges and that all government departments increase their hiring of blacks at professional levels.

The "moral leadership" on civil rights that Kennedy had promised during the campaign was an attempt to lead by example, not by new legislation or even speeches. This was perhaps impressive for 1961 or even in 1962, but by 1963 Kennedy himself learned that there was no time left.

The administration also tried to get J. Edgar Hoover's Federal Bureau of Investigation involved, and the agency accomplished more on civil rights than is commonly supposed. Hoover even transferred Southern-born agents out of Southern offices, for example. But he had a problem apart from his own conservatism and his strong belief in federalism: local police forces in the South were infiltrated by members of the Ku Klux Klan along with unaffiliated racists. Hoover's FBI had been careful to establish a cooperative relationship with local police that he did not wish to jeopardize. He had only a few blacks in his agency, among them his personal drivers and bodyguards; the Justice Department itself had only ten black lawyers out of some 1,000. Hoover was not the irresponsible psychopath television docudramas have made him out to be, and for many years the FBI maintained at least the appearance of a procedurally careful investigative force, a buttress rather than a threat to constitutional restrictions on federal power (privately Hoover had a habit of collecting potentially damaging information about politicians). It was a way of winning popular favor for the bureau: there are very few countries where the central police have enjoyed the public affection that the FBI received. But along with this carefully guarded demeanor went a temperamental stodginess that had little tolerance for public demonstrations, civil disobedience, and staged violations of social customs.

While Robert Kennedy pushed Hoover toward greater involvement in protecting civil rights workers and integrating the FBI, Hoover was able to convince the Justice Department civil rights lawyers, and through them the Kennedys, that Martin Luther King was consorting with known Communists. On learning this the president feared that an alliance with King would taint him with radicalism. He spoke to King in the White House Rose Garden in mid-1963 and warned him against his leftist friends as well as possible surveillance. The question revolved principally about a close friend of King, Stanley Levison, who had been very active in the Communist Party less than a decade earlier. Although there was no hard proof, the Justice Department thought Levison might have infiltrated the civil rights movement to promote communism. Subsequently, Hoover discovered that King was continuing his association with ex-communists despite his promise to the president. Because of King's refusal to desert Levison, the FBI, with permission from the attorney general, began monitoring King's private conversations in late 1963.

Hoover also monitored an affair between the president and a woman who was also the mistress of a prominent Mafia leader. After a warning from the FBI leader, the relationship between Kennedy and Judith Exner was abruptly terminated. James MacGregor Burns has written that public character "turns on criteria of persistence, commitment, courage. . . . In the old days, leadership related to a president's pursuing of lofty ends, as in the case of [Jefferson and Wilson]. More recently moral leadership has been defined more often as relating to the president setting some kind of personal standard of morality. . . . I believe that the former concept is the more relevant one." (Before he died in November 1963 Kennedy's very amorous life was confined to a Vassar graduate, Mary Pinchot of the Pinchot family reknown in American history. To her he revealed how much the word *liberal* made him gag. He apparently longed to be a college professor after his presidency, but the idea of associating with pretentious, pompous liberals deeply troubled him, he told her.) Kennedy, however, was a paragon neither in public or in private. He secretly tape recorded much of what was said in the Oval Office, unbeknown even to most of his closest advisers. He also ordered wiretaps on at least one congressman, and the administration prevailed on the Internal Revenue Service to audit groups it wanted to harass.

In 1963 the Kennedys were still signaling the South that they desired to maintain good relations at the same moment that the government was responding to blacks for almost the first time in nearly a century. The policy might have taken its natural course, with each small government gesture a step toward a formal reality the South could not avoid. But Southern bigots forced the administration to act directly against them.

After a federal court ordered state officials to admit James Meredith to the University of Mississippi in the fall of 1962, some 550 federal marshals were under siege in a pitched battle with hinterland rednecks. The Kennedys would have cooperated with any reasonable plan to admit Meredith, but Governor Barnett, at great risk to the peace and safety of the campus, tried to maintain his popularity with the state's voters. He told a crowd of 46,000 at the Old Miss football game, "I love Mississippi. I love our people. I love our customs." The football team participated in the subsequent rioting almost en masse. A confused retired army general, Edwin Walker, encouraged the rioters, having discovered a connection among communism, integration, and the fall of Western civilization. After the mob killed two people and wounded twenty-eight marshals with gunfire, the president responded by sending some 23,000 federal troops. There would probably have been more bloodshed had the president allowed the marshals to use their firearms, but Kennedy was finally doing what Eisenhower had done five years before at Little Rock. Soldiers would remain on the campus for months. At last it was definite and clear that the federal government would enforce the law. The Mississippi State Senate passed a toothless motion expressing its "complete, entire and utter contempt for the Kennedy administration and its puppet courts."

In the spring of 1963 federal soldiers also protected two students enrolling at the University of Alabama. Here the president acted more swiftly, this time against a segregationist governor, George Wallace, who knew that compromise need not destroy his reputation. Against the advice of his staff, the president spoke to the nation, again calling the matter of race a "moral issue," and as soon as Wallace had performed his ritual act of "standing in the schoolhouse door" Kennedy summoned the National Guard to ensure compliance. Some

375 business executives in Alabama were phoned for help in avoiding trouble. Robert Kennedy, in Alabama for a press conference, was asked if he was a member of the Communist Party and was jabbed with a nightstick by a state trooper.

Worse violence also came to Birmingham that same spring of 1963 when massive demonstrations by blacks for better jobs brought massive retaliation: electric cattle prods, police dogs, fire hoses. Burke Marshall, ever the negotiator, joined with other officials to win at least a part of the business community to the side of peace, but rioting meant that the civil rights movement had ended its nonviolent phase. Robert Kennedy objected to the protesters' use of children in their demonstrations, to which King countered that greater injury would come from continued discrimination. Soon violence would spread to the North, and the civil rights movement would lose much of its original nonviolent character.

On television an angry President Kennedy spoke eloquently and almost extemporaneously on morality and justice. Finally in full public support of the movement, he was a hero to most American blacks, although many black leaders and white allies thought his support came too late. In a 1963 poll blacks generally favored Kennedy against a Nelson Rockefeller Republican candidacy in 1964 by 89 to 3 percent and against the conservative Barry Goldwater by 91 to 2 percent. The supposed drift by blacks to the Republicans under President Eisenhower had been stemmed.

The White House sent Congress its first civil rights bill in February 1963, before Birmingham. It was a very weak measure, but at last the nation's president was plainly calling race discrimination wrong. Most of his advisers, including Vice President Johnson, thought the new bill could not pass. But in 1963 Kennedy worked hard to enact civil rights legislation, strengthening it enormously after riots in Birmingham by adding a ban on discrimination in public accommodations. Even voting rights provisions were included, but they did not become law until 1965. Mississippi's Senator James Eastland termed the bill a "complete blueprint for a totalitarian state." The president enlisted not only Johnson's help but also that of Representative Charles Halleck and Senator Everett Dirksen, the two Republican leaders in Congress. When Dirksen agreed in November not to support a filibuster, passage of a bill seemed certain, though a sizable minority of House Republicans opposed it. Before Kennedy's assassination the House Judiciary Committee had cleared the bill for a vote. Almost all members of Congress received pleas from the White House to favor the bill, and the president spoke with groups of national business, religious, legal, and labor leaders who might aid in its passage. If moderate blacks did not achieve what they legitimately wanted, the Kennedys warned, extremist groups would win civil rights leadership. Robert Kennedy repeatedly urged a new law to get black protesters "off the streets and into the courts." Southerners like Johnson and Dean Rusk of Georgia pleaded with wavering senators.

The laws that passed in 1964 and 1965 went farther than the president's bill, but the Kennedys labored hard for civil rights in 1963, and they began to lose some public support on it. Twice as many Americans thought that the administration was moving too fast as thought its progress too slow, and Kennedy's popularity plummeted throughout the white South where in June he received only a 33 percent approval rating. His likely opponent Goldwater did well in the South in 1964, and a chilly reception for the president in Philadelphia the year before had given premonitions of a white backlash in the North. The administration feared that King's March on Washington scheduled for August 1963 might turn violent, giving the South the chance to argue that it was being threatened by unruly mobs.

Failing the previous June to get the march canceled, the White House embraced it. "I'll look forward to being there," the president said at his July 17 presidential news conference, and the administration persuaded the theologically conservative Roman Catholic archbishop of Washington, Patrick O'-

Boyle, to attend. As the day of the march approached one of its leaders said of Kennedy: "He almost smothered us [with support]. We had to keep raising our demands to keep him from getting ahead of us." The march was a heartening gathering of a quarter million blacks and whites—the largest crowd ever to assemble in American history. Joan Baez sang "We Shall Overcome" and then joined Peter, Paul, and Mary in a moving rendition of Bob Dylan's "Blowin' in the Wind." Dylan, Odetta, and Mahalia Jackson also performed. The president met afterward for coffee in the White House with ten major black leaders, recalling his serving coffee to a group of pacifist picketers in front of the White House during 1961.

On August 28 King delivered his famous and moving "I Have a Dream" speech, which was a counterpoise to the ugliness and violence of Birmingham. "I have a dream," he orated, "that one day . . . when we let freedom ring, when we let it ring from every village and every hamlet, from every state and every city, we will be able to speed up that day when all God's children, black men and white men, Jews and Gentiles, Protestants and Catholics, will be able to join in the words of that old Negro spiritual 'Free at last. Free at last, Thank God almighty, we are free at last.'" John and Robert Kennedy had not really joined him in visualizing that dream, but the white South and most of the nation's blacks saw them in league. Their approaches differed. The Kennedy brothers believed in a gradual, incremental resolution of issues in preference to dangerous confrontation. Robert particularly favored federal pressure, a strategy-tempered idealism. The right to vote, the president and his attorney general thought, would be the most effective goal. Liberals in Congress, a memoir by Robert Kennedy observes, preferred failure to a reasonable bill: "An awful lot of them, as I said then, were in love with death." They thought only of their own goals, he wrote, rather than of the needs of others or of practical problems. This moralistic denunciation of moralistic liberals came from a man in whom virtuous anger seemed always close to the surface. Quite possibly a desire to go beyond practical limits might have had the effect of widening them. But Robert Kennedy made a good case against the virtuousness that thirsts after purity, even at the cost of defeat. The Kennedys believed in a federal power that could be used calculatingly against racism. It was the task of the Kennedy administration, more than of any other in the history of civil rights, to act for that part of the democratic process that restrained an unjust popular will.

Hesitancy not only kept the Kennedys from full participation in the largest movement of their time for social justice but also marked their temperamental distance from its peculiar character, a character that is as important morally as its technical goals. The civil disobedience and the peaceful walks through angry crowds were more than protests against segregation. They were in themselves acts of spiritual integration, a stepping through the violence of the mob and of the racist tradition. They repressed the human urge to violence within the protesters themselves and instead emphasized peace and civility.

The rights demonstrators also raised questions of confrontation between law and conscience. That confrontation was not sharp and absolute, since the rights forces claimed (correctly) to be working to enforce the Constitution. But in style and sometimes in substance they were making a choice for conviction and against the immediate agents of legal authority. The peaceful act of conscience in the face of law or custom had an ancestry in abolitionism. But in more recent times the notion had nearly atrophied. The civil rights movement reawakened it, the antiwar protests nourished it, and it remained a dilemma for a small but significant number of Americans who had to learn that conscience may simultaneously require the upholding of a system of laws and yet the defiance of an unjust law.

The Kennedys were outside all this, although Robert would

later acquire some affinity with the antiwar movement. But an administration is the sworn defender of institutions; it is supposed to respect informal political procedures, effect compromises, and preserve tranquility. The Kennedy presidency was behaving within that understanding of its role. In so doing, it succeeded in translating into some solid policies and laws the objectives of a movement that looked beyond law and policy to the uncompromisable demands of justice.

VIII

Now We Are All Keynesians

KENNEDY HAD BECOME president with little established ideological character beyond some unobtrusive movement toward Democratic liberalism in the late 1950s. In an article for *Life* in March 1960 he defined his party's problems in acquiring political identity. He argued that Eisenhower, on the moderate side of traditional Republicanism, had left the Democrats with little room in which to maneuver. If they too occupied the center, they would have little political distinctiveness. If they moved to the left as the times seemed to dictate, they would risk losing both the conservative and the moderate Southerners whom they needed to remain a strong national party. For Democrats that basic problem had long existed: in this century the conservative South and the liberal North have been antagonists, and only a national leader able to bridge those factions could bring the party to countrywide strength, an FDR or a Harry Truman, a John Kennedy or a Lyndon Johnson.

The article in *Life*, criticizing the nineteenth-century Whigs for lacking political identity, urged Democrats to press for an extension of their New Deal heritage. Shrewdly, however, Kennedy insisted that such programs were now the property of the political center, Southern and Northern, Republican and Democratic: his party therefore should seize the opportunity and take credit for adopting programs that Americans were ready for. Only in its advocacy of a form of Medicare does the article move in advance of what Kennedy regarded as the new political consensus.

In the spirit of the *Life* article the presidential candidate's campaign speeches lacked a definite ideology. That is one reason it was not odd for Kennedy to be in tandem with Lyndon Johnson, who was not identified with the politics of the deep South and who, having a long loyalty to the New Deal, could return to his political roots toward the end of the 1950s. Their opponents in the campaign, Richard Nixon and Henry Cabot Lodge, Jr., espoused the same brand of moderate politics. On the Democratic side, the confident rhetoric of the candidates suggested that they had a definite platform and definite goals, even in speeches that yielded little in the way of specifics. Kennedy's brisk assertiveness in the television debates with Nixon especially cast him as a purposeful, independent figure who knew where he stood.

Although the campaign did not produce well-defined issues separating the candidates, Kennedy was implying something different in his repeated promise to get the country moving again. He was, perhaps half consciously, coupling a stimulative economic policy to the need to establish a worldwide American presence in confronting communism. Kennedy's liberalism seemed plainly subsidiary to the overriding goals of maintaining American prestige. If, for example, signing a loyalty oath to get a student loan might somehow jeopardize the country from getting the kind of brains it needed for its scientific competition with the Soviet Union, then he would vote, as he did in 1959, against such an oath. He visualized world politics as an athletic contest and ideology as only a tactic in winning the game. Certainly he shuddered at self-conscious compassion. Liberals of that stripe had frequently attacked his father, and by implication his whole family, for crudity. "I'm not comfortable with those people," he once said of the liberal Americans for Democratic Action. He brought to the presidency his preoccupation with winning and self-discipline, his Democratic credentials capped by dry reserve and fundamental good will. Then events slowly drove him leftward, most notably in the civil rights movement but also in economic thinking.

The way for congressional legislation was cleared by Speaker of the House Sam Rayburn on the last day of January 1961. The experienced Mr. Sam rammed through, by a slim five-vote margin, the enlarging of the House Rules Committee so that it could no longer bottle up liberal legislation. The president's vigorous state of the union address the day before assured the nation that there would be new efforts in foreign policy. But what about domestic needs? In that area the programs that Kennedy presented to Congress were highly conventional extensions of the New Deal welfare state: $5 billion for urban renewal housing projects, funds for retraining in areas of high unemployment (the Manpower Development and Training Act of 1962), increased funds for treating water pollution, aid for businessmen who would locate in depressed areas (the Area Redevelopment Bill of 1961), food stamps, an increased minimum wage, an easing of eligibility for Social Security, the Peace Corps, greater mental health spending, a Cape Cod National Seashore, an Arms Control and Disarmament Agency, and Medicare. Except for Medicare all of these proposals became law under Kennedy. Perhaps he would have done more if Rayburn had lived beyond 1961 when he was replaced by the less effective John McCormack of Massachusetts. McCormack did not get along with the president and even teamed with Representative James Delaney of New York City and influential Republicans to bury Kennedy's attempt to keep more public funds from parochial schools. In the Senate the powerful Lyndon Johnson was succeeded as Democratic leader by the less effective Mike Mansfield. Without Rayburn or Johnson to help in Congress, the president alone had to coax support from conservative Democratic leaders like Senator Robert Kerr of Oklahoma, a slow and cumbersome process for which Kennedy sometimes lacked patience. Some Democrats, like Wilbur Mills of the Ways and Means Committee, even found the White House "timid."

Questions have been raised about how effective Kennedy's programs, embodying party policy advanced by Democrats in the 1950s, really were. Free market advocates have argued that raising the minimum wage eliminates jobs for the poor: employers would close down or substitute machines for workers. Perhaps so, but a submarginal wage for adults is an evasion of the modern welfare state's responsibilities. Area redevelopment, offering cheap federal loans to potential employers and providing grants to municipalities, is another favorite target of free market economists; they charge that excessive attention to families with deep attachments to their region threw money away in areas once thriving but since weakened by depletion of resources or shifts in markets. Few jobs, in fact, came out of the program, and most of the money went to Democratic congressional districts. Lyndon Johnson's well-funded poverty program, the Economic Opportunity Act of 1965, followed much the same guidelines with uncertain results. The Omnibus Housing Act of 1961, which appropriated $2 billion for urban renewal, often substituted middle-class housing on sites hitherto occupied by slums. Congenial ethnic neighborhoods with strong family bonds were often damaged in the process. But millions of families earning below a living wage also came to occupy the new buildings. The Manpower Development and Training Act, which was to retrain workers displaced by automation, merely retrained workers for other entry-level jobs. Without adequate basic education to start with, the trainees wound up only slightly better off than before. The one measure that might have helped such people, aid for education, was derailed because the bishops of the Catholic Church decided to kill it rather than be excluded from its benefits. Still, all the programs were at least susceptible to standard conservative criticisms: perversion by bureaucrats, both in Washington and in large cities; violation of market logic; and favoritism to special interests.

The measure that generated wide interest over the years was the Juvenile Delinquency and Youth Offenses Control Act of 1961. The agency it established was run by a childhood friend of Robert Kennedy, David Hackett, upon whom the novelist John Knowles patterned the daring athlete-hero of *A Separate Peace*. All this appealed greatly to the president who believed physical training would maintain individual and national vigor, making "a nation of spectators" into of a "nation of participants." Hackett, a sort of bureaucratic guerrilla, took charge of an entity called the President's Committee on Juvenile Delinquency, which never met formally. He recruited Lloyd Ohlin, research director of the Columbia School of Social Work, and his colleague Richard Piven to set up a series of Mobilization for Youth cadres in cities. The idea was to test whether, after having their expectations raised, slum kids could be enticed into legitimate opportunities for social advancement rather than turning to crime if they had no recourse to other avenues of success. Most cities created nonprofit private corporations, bringing together social workers, college teachers, and private and public civic leaders to bypass the middle-class curricula of schools that shunned slum students and encouraged failure; the public welfare departments that robbed families of dignity and stability; and city government that provided services of poor quality except for police who acted an instruments of social control. Robert Kennedy in particular came to see the difference in the justice process for poor people versus those of stable means. He established within the Justice Department an Office for Criminal Justice to ensure free counsel for poor defendants. In 1963 the president introduced a proposed criminal justice act "to assure effective legal representation for every man." *The*

Other America, Michael Harrington's stirring discovery of the poor, got through to the conscience of the Kennedys; the violence of black demonstrations made its separate argument for relieving poverty.

During the president's final months plans were being considered to make an antipoverty program the lynchpin of his 1964 campaign. During the 1960 contest the candidate had occasionally discussed poverty, once declaring that the "war against poverty" is not over. By 1963 the idea of fighting poverty with funds derived from a more expansive economy following a tax cut seemed politically eye-catching, and the president thought of dramatizing the issue by traveling through Appalachia. Most Southerners would not object to poverty funds since their region would benefit disproportionately. Actually, the administration envisioned only a several-hundred-million-dollar program. But it would be a coordinated assault, and the notion of poverty amid plenty would be the focus along with the social obligation of the rich to the poor. At Robert Kennedy's home, Hickory Hill, administration members fought it out. George Kennan said the poor would always be with us, but Robert Kennedy strenuously disagreed. On November 20, 1963, the president expressed reservations about concentrating on poverty alone in 1964 and thought something should be done for the middle class at the same time.

Action seemed remote. For one thing, Kennedy was occupied by a series of foreign policy crises far more wrenching than those of the Eisenhower years. He put domestic issues aside whenever he could. Secretary of Agriculture Orville Freeman has said the president was "restless and uncomfortable" when talking about farm issues. When Secretary of Health, Education, and Welfare Anthony Celebrezze tried to speak to him about new legislation, Kennedy told him to go away: "You were the mayor of a large city. You know how to handle these problems. Now handle them." Celebrezze did, holding a famous press conference that focused on the relationship between smoking cigarettes and cancer (during which he chain-smoked). Nor did the makeup of Congress invite bold legislation. Of the 261 Democrats in the House, 101 were Southerners, most of them conservatives. The new president did put his prestige on the line to enlarge the size of the House Rules Committee, where much important liberal legislation had previously been bottled up, but he won this contest so narrowly that he had little taste for more combat with Congress. The *Kiplinger Washington Letter* correctly predicted that Kennedy would "*step around*" domestic problems, waiting for better Democratic majorities.

Where possible the president preferred to achieve reform through executive action. The status of women in government improved under his administration after he directed the Civil Service Commission to open all jobs to both sexes and to begin special recruitment efforts aimed at women. Unlike Truman or Eisenhower, Kennedy was willing to appoint a President's Commission on the Status of Women, which was chaired by Eleanor Roosevelt until her death in 1962. To Kennedy, females were, apart from his fondness for them, another possible national resource for use in the competition with the Soviets. He raised the rank of the head of the Women's Bureau to assistant secretary of labor. Although he endorsed the equal rights amendment during the campaign, women were then much divided on whether to push for it. With the president's help they won an important legislative victory in the Equal Pay Act of 1963, the first federal antidiscrimination law enacted on their behalf and affecting private as well as public employers. Funding the first day-care centers since World War II also passed Congress that year.

Kennedy could see that one of several independent reasons why he had won the election was Eisenhower's failure to quicken the economy, despite the pleas of Nixon and his economic adviser Arthur Burns, when it slumped into a recession in 1960. Recognizing that without a depression to combat, a president who styled himself a Democratic liberal must rely on the cooperation of business to succeed, and Kennedy was cautious in proposing a plan to invigorate the economy. At first he did not have to do anything, because increases in Social Security payments and a rise in the minimum wage provided minor stimuli. But he prepared the way for economic reform by endorsing a corporate liberalism to provide an activist government that would protect and nourish American business. The president himself told an Eastern business audience that government and business, "far from being natural enemies . . . are necessary allies." Both depended on prosperity. But business was ideologically reflexive against a Democrat in the White House; Republicans could much more easily have engineered a stimulative, Keynesian tax cut like the one Kennedy proposed in January 1963.

Businessmen need not have worried. Except for some attempts at stronger regulations by Washington's regulative agencies and some of the attorney general's actions against price fixing, Kennedy's policies did not hurt businessmen. All presidents, Democrats included, are friends to business.

Kennedy's Secretary of Commerce, Luther Hodges, even favored right to work laws, which restricted the rights of unions to organize. Trusts did not much bother the Kennedy brothers either; their chief of the Justice Department's antitrust division prosecuted anticompetitive practices but left monopolies alone, as Eisenhower had done. The Kennedy administration gave American Telephone and Telegraph a monopoly over communications satellites, which accomplished spectacular feats in the short run but brought long-range technological stagnation. A similar favor gave the drug industry freedom to control prices in exchange for tighter restrictions on quality, which the vigilance of Senator Estes Kefauver had won. The Dupont Company also received special treatment. Newton Minow of the Federal Communications

Commission and Joseph Swidler of the Federal Power Commission sometimes successfully championed the public interest against the wishes of business.

Of enormous immediate benefit to corporations was Kennedy's investment tax credit, which passed Congress late in 1962, allowing businesses to deduct 7 percent of the cost of new investment. Meant to spur the economy, the write-off, though apparently effective in European economies, probably encouraged unproductive investments. Businesses also got more generous depreciation allowances for new plants and equipment. These changes saved business some 10 to 20 percent on tax returns. According to Treasury Secretary Douglas Dillon, the corporate tax reduction was to be accompanied by a later lowering of taxes on individuals as well. Another law of benefit to business, the Trade Expansion Act of 1962, gave the president power to end tariffs on certain items in negotiation with the European Common Market. This legislation reversed a ten-year trend toward restrictions on American commerce and temporarily improved the United States balance of trade payments. While the French veto on Britain's entry into the Common Market and exemptions for domestic oil and textiles weakened the legislation, the "Kennedy round" of trade talks nevertheless cut tariffs on a third of some 6,300 products, thus creating the most liberal trade conditions of the twentieth century. American tariffs dropped 64 percent, and industrial nations cut their duties on imports by a third. Kennedy's "Grand Design" for an Atlantic trading community was partially achieved. His legislative triumph, won by some timely domestic concessions for textiles, ended the acquiescence to European and Japanese discrimination against American goods in the 1950s, which had lost this country its dominant position in international commerce.

Relations between big business and the Kennedy administration roughened when the President's Council of Economic Advisers made prices and wages its central concern. The council proposed to mobilize public opinion on behalf of an

incomes policy of temperate price and wage behavior and issued guideposts to define temperance. If wages increased
with productivity, profits would remain constant, and business would not have to raise prices, thus avoiding inflation.
Since productivity had been rising at about 3 percent a year,
prices should rise no faster. Kennedy comprehended and was
acting on the relationship between productivity and inflation:
more productivity was the way to increase wages without causing inflation. The guideposts kept wage increases within the
scope of advances in productivity.

Wages and prices in the vital steel industry would have a
major effect on the rest of the economy. The administration,
through Labor Secretary Arthur Goldberg, exerted extraordinary pressure on unions to negotiate new contracts within
the guidelines. The steel union did so. But in April 1962
Roger Blough of U.S. Steel came to the White House and
handed Kennedy a copy of a press release saying his company's prices would exceed the guideposts. Most other big steel
companies also raised their prices.

The president was enraged and felt personally insulted. Believing that his office had been demeaned, he went on television the next day: "In this serious hour in our nation's history, when we are confronted with grave crises in Berlin and
southeast Asia . . . [and] asking reservists to leave their homes
and families for months on end and servicemen to risk their
lives . . . , the American public will find it hard, as I do, to
accept a situation in which a tiny handful of steel executives
whose pursuit of private power and profit exceeds their sense
of public responsibility can show such utter contempt for the
interests of 185 million Americans." The Justice Department
convened a grand jury to investigate price fixing and suggested that more generous depreciation allowances for the
steel industry be repealed; Congress was persuaded to launch
an investigation; the Federal Trade Commission went on the
alert; the Pentagon canceled steel purchases from companies
that had raised their prices. Most newspapers criticized this

display of presidential power, failing to note that Blough himself had misused the government for his own advantage.

Fortunately for Kennedy, smaller steel companies had not yet increased prices, and Inland Steel, aware of insufficient demand for its product, announced it would hold the price line. Bethlehem Steel then rescinded its increase, and Blough surrendered. He had blundered. Raising prices was poor strategy at a time when European competitors already were selling at prices 30 percent under American companies, and soon the steel industry actually cut prices to ensure greater competition. What Kennedy did took courage, since it jeopardized the alliance that he needed to secure tax reform. His widely reported remark that his father had been right to call big businessmen "sons of bitches" further alienated business: the public did not learn that he had added "pricks" and, of oil and gasmen, "robbing bastards." He told Adlai Stevenson he would not again appear before the United States Chamber of Commerce, and he remarked, correctly, "I'm beginning to sound like Harry Truman." He was angered most not by the economic damage—a similar steel price raise sailed through a year later—but by the damage Blough could have done to his reputation as a political mediator. Kennedy was ever the politician.

Worse soon followed. The stock market plummeted in May 1962 in the largest one-day drop since the Great Depression. In a month the Dow Jones average fell by 27 percent. Corporate leaders blamed the troubles on Kennedy's confrontation with Blough. The president thereupon gave up on courting business and decided to push hard for the Keynesian policies of tax relief that Walter Heller, chairman of his Council of Economic Advisers, had convinced him would stimulate the economy and increase revenues. Beginning in 1961 Heller directed his Council to work for the realization of Truman's Employment Act of 1946, which called for "full employment." Keynes believed that capitalism could work well if government used its power to regulate the money supply together with its power to tax and spend. Since Keynes pushed for a more efficient operation of capitalism, it is strange that his ideas were popular only among liberals. And it was as a liberal now that Kennedy turned to Keynesianism.

Kennedy first pitched his brand of Keynes to a Yale University commencement audience in June 1962. He began by attacking a series of what he defined as economic myths, explaining, for example, that the federal debt was growing smaller as a proportion of gross national product. Then he appealed to business hardheadedness: "What is at stake in our economic decisions today is not some grand warfare of rival ideologies which will sweep the country with passion but the practical management of a modern economy." It was typical of him to ask for a "sober, dispassionate, and careful" dialogue to seek "technical answers" about how best to shape the national economy. The Yale audience was noncommittal. Later that year Kennedy found a more receptive crowd for his and Heller's conservative Keynesianism at the Economics Club of New York. Sounding conservative notes, he promised that his tax bill would increase profits, hold the deficit in bounds, soon generate surpluses, and avoid inflation. He discovered that many members of the managerial elite were ready for a careful sprinkling of Keynesianism. And Kennedy was careful: to avoid deficits any higher than Eisenhower's, he would phase in the tax cut over a three-year period. That won him the critical support of Virginia's influential fiscally conservative Senator, Harry Byrd. Actually many sophisticated businessmen were already convinced long before Kennedy's speech. The tax cut the president wanted would increase profits. The only question was over how the cut would be apportioned among the sectors of the economy. Kennedy's scheme was sufficiently balanced in favor of the less affluent to make it definable as liberal. Yet some liberal economists dissented. John Kenneth Galbraith, Kennedy's ambassador to

India, argued that the plan omitted adequate spending in the public sector—for better hospitals, universities, highways, and the like. The socialist Michael Harrington dubbed the Kennedy plan "reactionary Keynesianism." And the conservative Milton Friedman warned that the cut would not stimulate the economy.

Concurrently, Republican Treasury Secretary Dillon, son of a self-made Wall Street banker, proposed as a complement to the cut a tax code free of economically unproductive loopholes and special preferences that distorted the natural flow of investment. It was much the same proposal that Ronald Reagan would magisterially sweep through Congress a quarter century later. Attaching these reforms to the tax cut package in 1963, however, had the effect of stalling the bill. Lobbyists swarmed in Washington to defend special interests. By September the bill's chances for success brightened; everyone, it seemed, was greedy for a tax cut, and Dillon's reforms proved to be the price the administration had to pay for tax reduction. Passage in the House assured its adoption by the Senate where Senator Paul Douglas's $6 billion tax cut bill of 1958 had lost 65 to 23. Three months after Kennedy's assassination it passed overwhelmingly, with most of the loopholes unclosed and with some liberalization by President Johnson. It was a grand success. Gross national product shot up, and unemployment sank to 4.1 percent. The whole country was now Keynesian. Whether the tax cut also brought on the subsequent inflation or whether that resulted more from Johnson's attempt to provide both guns and butter—the Vietnam war and the Great Society—is still being debated. But the Kennedy record in economics appears strong: even before the tax cut, the real growth rate was 5.7 percent, unemployment 5 percent, and inflation 1.3 percent. The growth rate under Eisenhower was 2.3 percent.

By the end of his thousand days Kennedy was fast on his way to becoming a good Keynesian. He told Arthur Schlesinger in November 1963 that he was planning to announce in his state of the union address a comprehensive scheme for an assault on poverty. Probably it was the civil rights movement and the attendant unrest, perhaps it was also the confrontation with business or the effect the tax issue had on his thinking, that brought him to this decision. In economics as in issues of rights, Kennedy moved ideologically at the press of unforeseen events. Then on November 22 he went to Dallas.

I X

"The Torch Is Passed"

IN DALLAS ON November 22, 1963, President Kennedy planned to deliver a speech boasting of the nation's increased military might and its unmatched nuclear arsenal. The Kennedy administration's confident energies were appropriate to Dallas, which had produced a civic life on a grand scale. The building of the ultramodern airport shared with Fort Worth and the football stadium nearby at Irving express a strong, modern America much as the Kennedy forces sought for the country at large. In the scheduled talk the president also planned to warn of the world's dangers and to urge care in the deployment of nuclear weaponry. The speech was written to embody the mind of the speaker, spanning his earlier militancy and his more recent championship of coexistence, capturing the sense that the precise deployment and the precise restraint of power are the selfsame act of a tempered will.

Lee Harvey Oswald offers a profile of the lonely assassin driven by secret ambition for triumph and fame, lacking the perception and the discipline to endure life amid the dissatisfactions, the uncertainties, and the half-successes of human existence. Despising the waywardness of life, he lived in wayward response to appetites and sporadic plans.

Oswald's father died before he was born, and his mother went to work, leaving him on his own. He dominated her and was often truant, never graduating from high school though he was bright. A schoolmate has recalled Oswald's sad early years: he "seemed to be a boy that was looking for something to belong to, but I don't think anybody was looking for him to belong to them." Oswald had a brief, unsatisfactory stint in the marines, where he told one of his roommates that one day he would do something "really big." In the Marine Corps he received instruction in firing an M-1 rifle similar to the gun found with his fingerprints on it near the Texas Schoolbook Depository window. As a marine he became a marksman competent enough to shoot the president.

Those with no faith in the provisional orderings that life often assumes, or no patience for achieving them, may seek explanations and orderings that are grand and encompassing. Oswald became a Marxist. After he served in the Marine Corps, he visited the Soviet Union, where he asked for asylum to live with his Russian bride. There he could not use a rifle freely, as he had during his youth. He was compelled to join a hunting club and use a small shotgun under close supervision. Dissatisfied with such constraints in the Soviet Union, he then sought to live in Cuba, but officials there, like the Soviets, were unwilling to grant him citizenship.

Oswald's first attempt at glory was to fire on the Dallas home of General Edwin Walker, who kept a large billboard on his front lawn displaying anticommunist slogans. Oswald missed but learned from the attempt to fire two or three shots, not just one—and he practiced shooting his mail-order rifle as often as he could. From the window of the building where most investigators believe he was located, the first shot missed Kennedy entirely; the second, from a range of 190 feet with a telescopic lens, hit the president at the top of the spine and also injured a passenger; the third killed Kennedy instantly.

People living then remember what they were doing that afternoon when they heard the news. Gloria Steinem, a feminist leader not usually given to sentimentality, remembers, "I was walking, and I could see who knew and who didn't"; it was "like the future died." The Dallas police arrested Oswald within hours of the shooting. Then, in a bizarre twist, Jack Ruby, a nightclub owner friendly with the local authorities, passed by the prisoner in a crowded room, and shot and killed him. Ruby later died of cancer in prison. On such events conspiracy theories thrive, and books propounding notions of multiple assassins have flourished.

Kennedy, whose favorite poem was Alan Seeger's "I Have a Rendezvous with Death," had tempted death in Dallas; he courageously—and foolishly, recalling his risk-taking in World War II—rode with his wife in an open car through the streets of a city seething with anger over desegregation. Had he kept the plastic bubble on his car, the bullets could not have penetrated.

Oswald had been solitary all his life. As a teenager he told a psychiatrist that he "did not need any help from anybody." His wife Marina, when asked whether he might have worked with others, replied, "Never, Lee was too secretive ever to have told anyone his plans. Nor could he have acted in concert, accepted orders, or obeyed any orders or plans by anybody else." Oswald had little use for the opinions of others. "He trusted no one," Marina Oswald declared. Had Oswald been part of some grand conspiracy, involving Cuba, the Soviet Union, or the Central Intelligence Agency, he would not have shot at General Walker and thereby risked being eliminated from any future attempt on Kennedy's life. Nor would he have used low-quality mail order weaponry. Even the ammunition was cheap. The mount on the telescopic sight was held on by two screws set in shallow holes. The whole job was improvisation, not conspiracy.

A report on Kennedy's assassination, prepared by a commission under the direction of Chief Justice Earl Warren, concluded that Oswald had acted alone. The Warren Commission's work was flawed partly because explicit photographs and X-rays of the president's bloody remains had been withheld, at the family's request, from doctors performing an autopsy. Rather than settle questions, the report tantalized habitually suspicious minds. Some thought that because it was a government-sponsored investigation, it was designed to cover up a CIA plot. For others the quest for unanswered questions may have been just one more way to deal with grief. To raise new theories about the deaths of both John and Robert Kennedy "was a collective way of . . . greening . . . memories," Max Lerner suggests. Robert Kennedy himself did not accept a conspiracy explanation of his brother's killing: the fact of his brother's death overshadowed any effort to account for it.

Befitting her notion that Kennedy's presidency had been a time of grandeur and romance, a modern counterpart to King Arthur's Court at Camelot, Jacqueline Kennedy arranged a state funeral reminiscent of Lincoln's. Burial was on a hillside of Arlington National Cemetery overlooking the capital: a massive stone is carved with words from his inaugural address, and a perpetual flame burns at the site. A center for performing arts in the capital bears Kennedy's name, a memory of a presidency that was widely thought, somewhat in contravention of fact, to be a knowledgeable attendant upon the arts. Perhaps even more quickly than the assassinated Lincoln achieved transfiguration into a mythic embodiment of American purpose, President Kennedy was elevated in the national memory for his association with an especially gratifying moment in recent history, a time for the thawing of Cold War and the frozen customs of white supremacy. Yet like Lincoln he had moved cautiously toward some larger measure of racial justice. The world, claims the economist John Kenneth Galbraith in discussing the Kennedy legacy, received him as a warm, friendly, affirmative force. William Leuchtenburg tells of grief over the fallen Kennedy in Togoland and Bangladesh. For about a decade the polls that rank presidents placed Kennedy ahead of Franklin Roosevelt, and even in the 1980s two out of three Americans believed the country would have been much better off had Kennedy lived.

Initiator or not, [Kennedy in his final years lent to the moment a grace of figure and gesture and speech. The young looked to him as to few earlier presidents, and especially after his death. Government service and national pride suddenly took on a new appeal. The youth-oriented Peace Corps and its later domestic counterpart, VISTA (Volunteers in Service to America), championed by the attorney general, are familiar symbols of Kennedy's influence. The nation, or much of it, swelled with a somewhat naive pride at the handling of the missile crisis, the opening of a conversation with the Soviet Union, the victories over entrenched bigotry. Kennedy's words were often bolder than the deeds he could manage to accomplish. But words can be deeds. Like other actions, they transform consciousness, and in doing so may transform social fact. Kennedy's words, including his more militant statements, added gesture and moment to the beginnings of détente with Moscow; and his words reinforced a civil rights movement to which he had contributed no initiatives.] The Kennedys, Gore Vidal complained, "create illusions and call them facts." But the Kennedy legend created illusions and then helped to make them facts in the legislative achievements of Lyndon Johnson's administration.

After Kennedy died, ordinary Americans missed the high style that managed at once to convey courage, solemnity, and confidence. They also missed the warmth of a family in the White House, Caroline romping around in her mother's high heels, John-John running round and round his father's desk. They were not charmed by the new president who pulled his Beagle hound off the ground by his ears and assured onlookers it did not hurt the yelping dog. Memory conjured up a Camelot legend as well as dollar souvenir pictures of the martyred Kennedy with hands folded. Kennedy relished stark international dramas of confrontation, uncorrupted by ideological pronouncements, but he did not romanticize the daily business of politics and administration, and might have been surprised at his elevation in the American imagination. Yet his was a presidency that deserves recognition for its elusive qualities of style and purpose and even for its promised future. It is largely a matter of circumstance that a presidency which prided itself so much on level-headed solutions for domestic and foreign problems is now remembered for its high noons in the face of crises or its high-flown elocution. Kennedy himself was puzzled that historians ranked Woodrow Wilson above James Knox Polk or Harry Truman, because he believed that practical results counted more than high moral visions. A workaday speech delivered to the American Federation of Labor just before his death reflects that mentality: "No one gains by being admitted to a lunch counter if he has no money to spend. No one gains from attending a better school if he doesn't have a job after he graduates." Kennedy missed the point in both examples, as his own family's history demonstrated. The argument sounds conservative in its apparent subordination of issues of formal legislated racial equality. Yet it can also be read as a lesson in practical economic progressivism, in a tradition that has both accompanied and radically diverged from the upper middle-class priorities that are an element in twentieth-century liberalism. If Kennedy's comments are an expression on the one hand of his conservatism and skepticism toward social legislation, in another way they foreshadow the straightforward economic progressivism of Lyndon Johnson's presidency.

John Kennedy has been described as an English Whig "who believed that perfection is beyond us, that life was a comedy to those who think, a tragedy to those who feel." Everything in national life, Richard Rovere remarks, interested Kennedy, but it was an interest almost sardonic: "His zest for simply watching the show was as great as H. L. Mencken's. His curiosity seemed at times not only astonishing in itself but almost frivolous, almost perverse; he would spend time . . . talking and bothering about . . . the typography of a newspaper." He would not "think that everything would be Jim-dandy if we just had Medicare and stepped up production in our engineer factories, and got Negroes into nice, clean motels." Perhaps it is an irony, a detachment in Kennedy, that reconciles and explains the contradictory impressions of his intellect that observers have had. A skeptical mind can be very much alive to ideas, enjoy their play, and be deft at articulating them when the mood or the occasion demands. But it may also stop short of the full commitment that will issue in a finished book or essay a consistent political philosophy, a program defined and fought for over the course of a political career. Kennedy, for example, was more aware than the run of booster politicians that American schooling must be measured not only in quantity but in character. Rovere described a president engaged in details and aware of implications as well as a skeptic reaching for success and knowing that it would no doubt elude him. In his lack of enthusiasm for those reforms beneficial neither to the economy nor the poor, he might be placed to the left of conventional liberal concerns during the sixties. And his career set on course the leftward journeys of his brothers Robert and Edward.

John Kennedy's legacy has been argued over more than that of any other recent American president. His brothers, Robert and Edward, had influential careers that testify to the family's prominence. They also give hints of what kind of president John Kennedy might have become.

Robert, the sternest of the brothers, with a capacity for both moral arrogance and moral self-criticism, attended Harvard and, after brief service in the navy, completed his education at the University of Virginia Law School. There he wrote papers on the federal system, arguing against an overreaching national government. At Charlottesville he was outraged when, after he had invited the black statesman Ralph Bunche of the United Nations to speak, the university was unwilling to permit an integrated audience; he succeeded in getting

Virginia to allow the full audience. In the 1950s while he was working for Senator Joseph R. McCarthy's Permanent Senate Subcommittee on Investigations, Robert's moralism turned upon our ally Great Britain for trading with Communist China during the Korean War. His later explanation for supporting McCarthy was "I thought there was a serious internal security threat to the United States; I felt at the time that Joe McCarthy seemed to be the only one who was doing anything about it—I was wrong." By the late 1950s Robert, now in an equally angry pursuit of labor criminals, complained that the FBI was pursuing Communists with more vigor than it expended on gangsters.

Toward the end of John's Senate career, Robert worked with his brother in an investigation of the teamsters union, particularly Dave Beck and his successor Jimmy Hoffa. Beck went to prison; so did Hoffa until President Nixon pardoned him, after which Hoffa disappeared somewhere in New Jersey. Robert's energy spent itself effectively in the 1960 presidential campaign, and following long-range plans laid out by Joe Kennedy, Sr., he became attorney general in the new administration. Had President Kennedy, still timid about the racial issue, foreseen how large the issue would become, he might not have appointed his brother to an office so visibly central to the conflict. Later in the decade the same moral urgency that had fixed on anticommunism and warring against labor union corruption committed itself to a progressivism to the left of the conventional liberalism that Robert's elder brother had arrived at in his later days.

Robert's years in the Justice Department implicate him and his brother in a variety of controversial activities. Even as the attorney general led his brother toward activism in civil rights, he authorized, condoned, or overlooked wiretapping and led reckless undercover subversive efforts in Cuba. Elsewhere he permitted the training of foreign police forces in such skills as crowd control, pushing legal standards to limits outdistanced only by some of his successors. Convictions against organized crime went from 96 in 1961 to 373 in 1963. The nation paid for these convictions by unsettling infringements on civil liberties. And on the rights issue, Robert, like his brother, began by moving with events he had neither chosen nor desired. It took time for his touchy and unpredictable tendency to moral outrage to find this most valid of its objects. The initiative came from the black congregations and the Northern white freedom riders who made sure that the demand for civil rights did not settle into politically sedate requests. The Southern white mobs and law enforcement officials also played their unwitting part, acting as they and their ancestors had always acted, but doing so now before the national media and a public somewhat more enlightened in racial questions than it had once been. Still, the transformation of Robert Kennedy on civil rights was swifter and sharper than that of other advisers in the administration. As a force within the administration he and his department argued, for instance, that civil rights legislation should not await the enactment of tax reduction. And as the public came increasingly to perceive his office as a force within the civil rights movement and as white supremacists defined him as the enemy, his combativeness urged him further to identify with the cause.

Once Robert's consciousness was aroused, he became sharp, visceral, and explosive. The same fury he had once turned against allies who traded with Communist countries he now directed against those who had not arrived at his present sentiments on integration. With his friend David Hackett, he toured Harlem; and when he was away from cameras, with genuine unstrategic feeling he grabbed at the hands of little black children. His advanced progressivism began well before his brother's death, well before opportunism might have tempted him in search of presidential constituencies. He pushed hard while attorney general not only for legislation on VISTA but also for appropriations to combat juvenile delinquency and to nourish poverty programs. At a meeting of

Lyndon Johnson's committee against racial discrimination on May 29, 1963, Robert lost his temper at what he took to be lagging. "You mean," he shouted to James Webb of the National Aeronautics and Space Administration, that "you have 40,000 employees and one-and-one-half men working on this?" He swore at Webb, glared at Johnson, and stalked out. The committee had caught him at the wrong moment in his angry moral pilgrimage.

After President Kennedy's death many journalists spoke of a Kennedy dynasty, expecting Robert to become president, and perhaps Edward too. No friend of President Johnson, Robert moved to the Senate from New York and worked there for social reform. The new senator's pressing for domestic reform, and his transformation into a critic of the old ways of the Cold War, suggested that he was continuing the promise of his brother's administration: but that amounts to a retrospective bestowing on that administration of a meaning it had only begun to articulate. Latin American crowds cheered his populist rhetoric on trips there, and the local press lavished praise on his harsh criticism of the 1965 United States military intervention in the Dominican Republic. However, in 1961, during an earlier apparent crisis in that nation, he was contemptuous of a hesitancy to send troops there. "Large-scale land redistribution," Robert said in urging the Alliance for Progress to greater activity, "necessarily implies major changes in the internal political balance of many Latin American countries—away from oligarchy and privilege, toward more popular governments." He rebuked the Afrikaners for apartheid and told them about the success of the civil rights movement in the United States. He recoiled at the slaying of 100,000 Communists in Indonesia when most Americans were indifferent to the slaughter and a few were pleased at that country's rightward movement. Black Americans continued to trust the Kennedys. A youth, asked why Robert Kennedy's visit to his ghetto neighborhood could be such an event, replied, "His brother, the President, was like a father to me." But John Kennedy had taken a long time to assume fatherhood of a civil rights bill.

By the Democratic presidential primaries of 1968 Robert had moved to the far left of conventional politics. He identified himself not with some reformist impulse in the service of an undifferentiated national interest but with the needs and hopes of the poor and powerless. His opponent in the primaries, Eugene McCarthy, once spoke of blacks as "those people"—not with disrespect but merely with little feeling that they would have to be a major element in a successful Democratic campaign. But Kennedy remained a politician, and he remained within a general American consensus of values and manners. Although he abandoned the bland politics of the center, he did not endorse the scornful rejectionism of the New Left, at once elitist and militantly affirmative of the dispossessed. He now represented something that had nearly disappeared from American politics since the time of the New Deal: he was by and large a traditional economic and social insurgent, at a time when politicians like Hubert Humphrey were saying that the reforms of his generation had been accomplished and there was no need for more, while young leftists were scorning the traditional labor constituency and the welfare state.

There is no evidence that, however far to the left he had moved within the dominant American political spectrum, Robert Kennedy had ever abandoned the technocratic orientation of his brother's administration. He still perceived counterinsurgency as an alternative both to massive military involvement and to the surrendering of a Third World people to totalitarianism; but he would include within it a program for land reform, schools, clinics, unions—a program that would both gain the allegiance of the people and create a democratic progressivism worthy of victory. That program was the equivalent of the community action that Robert was proposing for domestic reform. And in the Kennedy manner and the spirit of mainline liberalism, it was a program demanding technical expertise.

In fact, Robert Kennedy was holding together the loosening strands of liberalism and progressivism, and soon after his death they unraveled further. Some liberals turned to an ecology movement that, though it employed experts, was hostile to the scientific and technological ethos that liberalism had trusted; Cold War liberalism confronted the antiwar movement; welfare-state policies argued with a left that preferred small-scale community; and the labor movement lost some of its force within the liberal alliance when the right won at least the momentary attention of blue collar workers.

Edward Moore Kennedy was the heir to the Kennedy legacy: "I don't think it's any mystery that I want to be President," he said as recently as 1982. But the self-destruction of liberalism, as well as his infamous automobile accident at Chappaquiddick Island, precluded his taking the presidential mantle. Since he did not reach the Senate until 1963, he lacks the contradictions of his two brothers, instead speaking consistently for a progressivism similar to Robert's in the late 1960s. Like his brother John, Edward is comfortable with the politicos; like Robert, he sincerely speaks a vocabulary of social justice. Events have granted him less glamour than his brothers acquired, yet he is in a number of ways the most solid of the three. He has shown more conscious social commitment than John had for most of his political life, and his manner has been more gracious and less bullying than Robert's was. He has demonstrated an ability to do standard legislative tasks with uncommon skill and in the interest of causes that his family, having come upon them gradually and circumstantially, can now still stubbornly serve.

To speak of the public that John Kennedy represented, the public that Robert and Edward Kennedy sought to reach, is to refer to two entities. Certain groups have formed the solid base of the family's power: blue-collar Democrats, liberal professionals, Catholic ethnics, blacks, Hispanics, Democratic leftists, and Democratic politicians who recognized President Kennedy as a politico. The Kennedys are associated also with a tone and persuasion that do not define any set of interest groups. John Kennedy was able to appeal to a range of Americans looking for something more visionary than conventional Democratic machine politicians could offer yet more solidly grounded in questions of labor and economics and even military preparedness than, say, the ecology movement would consider.

Kennedy liberalism, as articulated by Robert and Edward Kennedy, and even in the parallel progressive measures of Lyndon Johnson's administration, now has form and conviction. It was not until shortly before his death that President Kennedy momentarily held unchallenged a reputation for being a liberal. Civil rights and the test ban, and perhaps more particularly the right-wing denunciation of these actions, established his presidency among the forces for mild and consensual progress. The clear placement of his brothers in the left of the party solidified that impression, the more so since they conveyed the same feeling of energy and action that the public had gained from his person and administration. That there was from the beginning such a thing as Kennedy liberalism continues to be a popular conviction: in part because a portion of the right persists angrily in believing so. Kennedy's presidency also has had an able champion in Arthur M. Schlesinger, Jr., a historian and his White House adviser.

Schlesinger has spoken for a brand of liberalism that defines a recurrent progressive egalitarianism in American politics, one at war with privilege in differing forms and manifesting itself in this century most notably in the New Deal. *The Politics of Hope,* a collection of essays on American culture and politics that Schlesinger published before Kennedy's death, sides less with any one political or philosophical persuasion than with intellectual curiosity, skepticism, restlessness, and habits of mind that many commentators were perceiving as having atrophied in the complacencies of the nation's midcentury. For liberal intellectuals like Schlesinger, Kennedy's presidency meant the return of critical and experimental intelligence. The kinds of virtue that the essays prize call to mind another characteristic of liberalism that relates it both to modern technology and to the ambivalently liberal John Kennedy; that characteristic is a strenuous and unresting morality of problem solving, as opposed to a morality of conservation or a question of a permanent utopia.

A Thousand Days, Schlesinger's encyclopedic retrospective of the Kennedy administration published in 1965, chronicles the varying impulses of energy and reform that he finds there. The magisterial work presents Kennedy liberalism as another instance of a progressive American politics that rewins freedom and equality from reactionaries. The author's great constant is that a liberal will have an attitude that can be defined as compassionate, while a conservative will define it as hopelessly softminded and irresponsible. *A Thousand Days,* though often critical if read between the lines, stands as a memorial to the John Kennedy still so fresh in the public mind.

While this view of the Kennedy years has never disappeared, the Vietnam War severely threatened it. According to right-wing conservatives, Kennedy failed to follow through with devastating force after the Bay of Pigs, the Berlin Wall, the Cuban missile crisis, and the deposing of Premier Diem in Vietnam. But for the left Vietnam reveals the unspeakable truth about liberalism. The British writer Eric Hobsbawm, in an article entitled "Why America Lost the Vietnam War," labels Kennedy the "most dangerous and megalomaniac" of presidents. Vietnam was surely a liberals' war, an outcome both of the Cold War commitments under President Truman and of the more general Wilsonian determination to have this country sustain major responsibilities abroad. Yet liberalism ripped itself to shreds over the conflict. By the time that much of the left community had turned against this war, the Kennedy administration as a promoter of the military mind and a contributor to our commitments in Southeast Asia was vulnerable to reappraisal. The war, moreover, in conjunction with the fundamental critique of American society that was implicit in the civil rights movement, modified the character of public debate. For the first time in many years, a radical commentary addressed the issue of how far capitalism should temper itself with a welfare state. Scholars proposed that the Cold War was not merely a Western response to Stalinist ambitions but in part an aggressive American pursuit of economic interests and mindless anticommunism. Disaffected radicals attacked the welfare state as a capitalist strategy for buying the poor or for controlling them. By such reckonings it was no longer a question of whether John Kennedy was a good liberal. Liberalism itself was now under attack as a sophisticated form of political reaction.

In fact, in recent years, it has become common to perceive conservatism or reaction in presidents who in earlier generations were perceived as liberals. Theodore Roosevelt's imperialist emotions now appear as an inseparable component of his brand of progressivism. Woodrow Wilson has become identifiable with the racial segregation of federal workers and the achievement of a liberal capitalist world order under American hegemony. Franklin D. Roosevelt is recalled as the paternal conservative, saving capitalism from its own politically self-destructive ruthlessness. Harry Truman is now remembered less for resisting congressional red hunts and more for presiding over a federal loyalty program. John Kennedy had not long been dead when his presidency, for reasons peculiar to it, underwent a similar reevaluation among many commentators.

Even Schlesinger in a mid-1980s symposium reflects on Kennedy's habit of operating out of channels and his "addiction to activism." The charge is also true of many other Democratic politicians of the day. Adlai Stevenson, for instance, wanted to send a United Nations force to the Congo in 1961. Under Kennedy the CIA had plans to rid Haiti of its dictator,

François Duvalier. Democratic internationalists did not generally believe it wise to let other countries pursue their own historical logic, especially if it included bloody civil strife.

Certainly the critics make a case that the Kennedy administration smacked of calisthenics and distance running in the cold. To what extent does the record really reflect the charge of reckless adventurism? Perhaps the case is really to be made against a liberalism that has lost confidence in its past, a liberalism at odds with itself. Its driven conscience is irreconcilable with the permissiveness particularly of the 1960s; its wish for a more cooperative social order is mocked by its fascination with the claims of personal self-cultivation and privacy, most notably in the 1970s and after. Present-day conservatism is similarly contradictory when it gives individualist economics a vocabulary from a nineteenth-century European ideology of order, place, and hierarchy.

A temperate critique of Kennedy is Henry Fairlie's *The Kennedy Promise*, published in 1973. Fairlie, a British-born political columnist, does not share in the anti-Americanism that attended the attack on this nation's foreign policy. Combining a social democratic persuasion with an intellectual conservative's preference for good manners and rigorous morals, he has observed with sympathy and respect the trials his adopted home has passed through in recent decades. *The Kennedy Promise* does not totally reject American Cold War principles. Fairlie's claim that American aid in the early postwar years helped save western Europe from Stalinism, and did so with good intentions, is rather a dissent from the dissent that other recent opponents of American foreign policy have engaged in.

The mistake of the Kennedy administration, Fairlie argues, was to go beyond the essentially defensive and stabilizing policies of restraining Communist expansionism and instead to make war with guerrillas in regions where conditions and issues were beyond our comprehension. Fairlie believes that by waging guerrilla warfare against communism, Kennedy undermined the legitimacy of earlier attempts to stabilize world order; Fairlie places the blame on almost exactly what some admirers of John Kennedy have lauded: the idea that energy and action are inherently good qualities. Essentially, Fairlie's views represent a conservative's argument on the left.

Garry Wills has been ranked among twentieth-century American conservatives, and even after the distance between him and conventional commentators on the right became apparent, he was reluctant to surrender the label of conservative. His *The Kennedy Imprisonment,* published in 1982, is an illustration of the passing or at any rate the softening of the terms that once distinguished left from right in conventional American politics. Defining the vice of the Kennedy administration as the elevating of will and power to ends in themselves, *The Kennedy Imprisonment* is, among other things, an attack on the pretensions and the power hunger of the presidential office. If a book arguing that thesis had appeared during Franklin Roosevelt's administration, it would almost certainly have been a conservative lament, inasmuch as the assault on the New Deal was largely an assault on what conservatives saw as a massive growth in federal power centered in the presidency. But the arrogance of White House functionaries in the Nixon and Reagan administrations later turned many on the left into partisans of Congress. Wills's description of Kennedy's presidency makes it sound remarkably like the office that its staff and unofficial shock troops in the recent Republican years of Nixon and Reagan have made it into: overgrown pride over its might and mysteries and prerogatives, disdainful of procedures, relishing swift guerrilla tactics among its strutting operatives in aid of privately conceived projects. The question of how much power the White House should have is, of course, not quite so philosophically compelling as are questions of how wealth should be distributed or American resources deployed abroad. It is to be expected that the next equivalent of a New Deal president will enlist descendants of twentieth-century liberalism on the side of the executive branch, while any future president who offers vigorous support to progressive movements abroad will turn right-wingers into defenders of congressional privilege. But Wills is interested in issues of power and procedures as issues in themselves, and his preferences for steady, formally established ways of governing allies him to conservatism in its liking for customs and institutions, and to liberalism in its suspicion of emotion and willfulness.

Nancy Gager Clinch's *The Kennedy Neurosis,* published in 1973, is an example of the extremes of criticism John Kennedy has received. The book defines a neurosis in the Kennedy family as only an accentuation of an illness in the country as a whole. Pressed by Joe Kennedy, Sr., to an obsession to achieve, repeatedly confronted by their father with their failure to satisfy him, the Kennedy brothers have been compelled toward both success and self-punishment, along with a stunting of emotions. Thus the adventurism in foreign policy combined with an inability to recognize, say, the experience of poverty. In the manner of much psychohistory, the author analyzes without the benefit of continuing private access to the patient. Nor will she allow her subjects what people who go before a public are generally granted: to be loved or hated or tolerated for the public selves they construct. The book is a polemic. The author attacks her subject with the criteria that are at anyone's verbal command: emotional instability, sexual irregularity, hidden rage, lack of self-esteem, and so on. But the polemic does raise the unavoidable question of whether American culture is fixed to competitiveness and self-punishment at the expense of a larger range of experience and emotions, and the author simply uses the Kennedy family as a model, to be assented to or rejected, for the understanding of the American character.

John Kennedy has been subjected to the conflicting evaluations that scholars and other commentators devise for any person, period, or movement. If the clash in interpretation has occurred sooner after the event than is usual in the reappraisal of the past—sooner than, say, FDR the advanced reformer became FDR the patrician conservative—it is partly because so much happened so quickly to political debate in the unsettling late 1960s, and partly because Kennedy's administration was in fact so elusive of definition, at once so emphatic in its sense of energy and so unclear in the direction of that energy.

One testimony to the way that President Kennedy has entered the American public mind is the recent invoking of his memory on the part of Democratic politicians. In the 1988 presidential race, for example, the various Democratic candidates have saluted him, the old cadences and phrases serving as a bridge to the future. Senator Richard Gephardt of Missouri reminded his audiences of Kennedy's promise to put a man on the moon and offered his own variant: striking chords that Kennedy sounded, Gephardt would make Americans "the best educated and trained people on the face of the earth." In a call to worldwide competition, he urged his listeners: "We can do it. Remember Sputnik." Senator Joseph Biden of Delaware, who withdrew early from the race under fire for plagiarism, paraphrased Kennedy's inaugural address: "In the spirit of another time, let us pledge that our generation of Americans will pay any price, bear any burden, accept any challenge, meet any hardship to secure the blessings of prosperity and the promise of America for our children." Governor Michael S. Dukakis of Massachusetts implicitly compared Ronald Reagan's appeal to selfishness in 1980, "Are you better off than you were four years ago?" to Kennedy's "Ask not what your country can do for you—ask what you can do for your country." Dukakis phrased it: "Ask more of your candidates, because the next President will be asking more of you." All of these candidates and others echoed Kennedy's "new generation" theme. Dukakis often mentioned that it was because of Kennedy that he entered public life, and once he wiped away tears when he dedicated a park to the slain president. Biden said that this generation had not forgotten its idealism or its "murdered heroes." "If you lived through it," recalled the national chairman of the Democratic party, Paul Kirk, the Kennedy era "was a call to greatness, it was the country feeling young and good about itself." All this strategy attempted to identify with a man who still ranks in most public opinion polls as the most popular American president.

Even conservatives call on the memory of John Kennedy. Congressman Jack F. Kemp, a Republican presidential contender in 1988, argued that "John F. Kennedy didn't just talk about researching and testing putting a man on the moon by the end of the decade. Ladies and gentlemen, we should not just research and test S.D.I. [Strategic Defense Initiative]. We should research, test and deploy S.D.I." Presidents Richard Nixon and Ronald Reagan have also fallen back on the martyred president for bits and pieces of their identities, emphasizing his Cold War initiatives.

John Kennedy has become the model of presidential style in the last part of the twentieth century. Unlike succeeding presidents he was not disgraced in his second term or rejected by the voters. He was the last President to project a speech and manner that kept their effectiveness to the end. But beyond the pleasant circumstances of the Kennedy presidency—the lucky clustering of events well suited to his manner and rhetoric, as well as initiatives such as the formation of the Peace Corps, that were chiefly of his making—are deeper and complex relationships between the Kennedys and the American experience.

There is the composite and contradictory twentieth-century American liberalism that the Kennedy politics managed to embrace over time. The militant Cold War liberalism that appointed John Kennedy its spokesman during the missile gap campaign turned to the liberalism of military disengagement and détente in 1963, well embodied in the test ban treaty and the American University speech. The liberal faith in the scientific and technological virtues—a tradition going back in time with the term "liberalism" through its varying and conflicting usages—had an appropriate figure in a president who urged investment in space and strove for a more elite and more technically sophisticated military. Meanwhile, it was his undesired good fortune to connect with a civil rights movement that expressed a morality not of technical planning and cautious exactitude but of spiritual witness and confrontation. The similarity between the domestic schemes for community action envisioned under Walter Heller in 1963 and the development of programs that Maxwell Taylor hoped would create anticommunist Vietnamese villages suggests the diversity of intentions within Democratic liberalism.

The Kennedy family too has been a composite in obvious and familiar ways: immigrant outsiders evolved into prominent Americans; Boston Irish becoming patricians; and aggressive entrepreneurs in business and politics transforming themselves into public-spirited if ambitious statesmen. The Kennedy family invented itself, quite determinedly in the case of John Kennedy, who was both the creature of his father's wishes and the product of his own will, asserted against continual illness. And in inventing itself, the Kennedy family has been the quintessence of a nation that, for good or bad, is a perpetual work of invention.

Bibliography

JOHN KENNEDY HAS had a fair-minded biographer in Herbert Parmet, whose two volumes were published by Dial Press in 1980 (*Jack: The Struggles of John F. Kennedy*) and 1983 (*JFK: The Presidency of John F. Kennedy*). Parmet gives no quarter on such sensitive topics as the Castro assassination plans but acknowledges Kennedy's abilities and idealism. Parmet's book does not supplant Arthur Schlesinger's *A Thousand Days* (Boston: Houghton Mifflin, 1965) written with the perspective of a contemporary and witness.

The most interesting development in the Kennedy literature has been a generation of highly critical "revisionist" commentary much influenced by the Vietnam War. Heralded in mature form with a 1966 article in *Commentary* by George Kateb, the Amherst College political scientist, the revisionist interpretation has continued at least until Garry Wills's 1982 *The Kennedy Imprisonment: A Meditation on Power* (Boston: Little, Brown). Its most restrained and complex example is by Henry Fairlie, *The Kennedy Promise: The Politics of Expectation* (Garden City, N.Y.: Doubleday, 1973), and its most polemical is by Nancy Gager Clinch, *The Kennedy Neurosis: A Psychological Portrait of an American Dynasty* (New York: Grosset & Dunlap, 1973). Other notable examples of the revisionist genre include Richard J. Walton, *Cold War and Counterrevolution: The Foreign Policy of John F. Kennedy* (Baltimore: Pelican Books, 1972); Louise FitzSimons, *The Kennedy Doctrine* (New York: Random House, 1972); Bruce Miroff, *Pragmatic Illusions: The Presiden-*

tial Politics of John F. Kennedy (New York: David McKay, 1976);
Thomas G. Paterson's "Bearing the Burden: A Critical Look
at JFK's Foreign Policy," *Virginia Quarterly Review,* vol. 54
(Spring 1978), pp. 193–212; and I. F. Stone, *In a Time of Tor-
ment* (New York: Random House, 1967). A muckraking study
is Victor Lasky, *J.F.K.: The Man and the Myth* (New Rochelle,
N.Y.: Arlington House, 1963; rev. ed. 1966).

A less articulate body of literature is composed of reminiscences by Kennedy's associates. The most knowledgeable are
two books by Theodore Sorensen: *Kennedy* (New York: Harper & Row, 1965) and *The Kennedy Legacy* (New York: Macmillan, 1973). Also useful are Kenneth P. O'Donnell and David F. Powers with Joe McCarthy, "'*Johnny, We Hardly Knew
Ye': Memories of John Fitzgerald Kennedy*" (Boston: Little Brown,
1972); Pierre Salinger, *With Kennedy* (Garden City, N.Y.: Doubleday, 1966); Lawrence F. O'Brien, *No Final Victories* (Garden
City, N.Y.: Doubleday, 1964); Paul B. Fay, *The Pleasure of His
Company* (New York: Harper & Row, 1966); Benjamin Brad-
lee, *Conversations with Kennedy* (New York: W. W. Norton,
1975); Evelyn Lincoln, *My Twelve Years with John F. Kennedy*
(New York: David McKay, 1965); and Edwin Guthman, *We
Band of Brothers* (New York: Harper and Row, 1971).

The abundant literature on Kennedy's prepresidential
years is nicely summarized in Herbert Parmet's *Jack.* Doris
Kearns Goodwin, the only scholar to have had access to Joseph and Rose Kennedy's papers, adds important detail in
her *The Fitzgeralds and the Kennedys: An American Saga* (New
York: Simon & Schuster, 1987). Joe Kennedy is studied in
Richard Whalen, *The Founding Father* (New York: New American Library, 1964); David E. Koskoff, *Joseph P. Kennedy* (Englewood Cliffs, N.J.: Prentice-Hall, 1974); and Michael R. Bes-
chloss, *Kennedy and Roosevelt: The Uneasy Alliance* (New York:
W. W. Norton, 1980). Rose Kennedy's reminiscences are entitled *Time to Remember* (Garden City, N.Y.: Doubleday, 1974).
A very important study of JFK's early years is Joan and Clay
Blair, *The Search for JFK* (New York: Berkley, 1976).

Each episode of Kennedy's foreign policy has generated a considerable analysis. On the first excursion: Peter Weyden, *Bay of Pigs* (New York: Simon and Schuster, 1979); Haynes Johnson, *The Bay of Pigs* (New York: Simon & Schuster, 1964); and the initial section of Irving Janis, *Victims of Groupthink* (Boston: Houghton Mifflin, 1972). Books specifically on Berlin include Honoré Marc Catudal, *Kennedy and the Berlin Wall Crisis* (Berlin: Berlin Verlag, 1980); Robert Slusser, *The Berlin Crisis of 1961* (Baltimore: The Johns Hopkins University Press, 1971); Curtis Cate, *The Ides of August: The Berlin Wall Crisis of 1961* (New York: M. Evans, 1978); and Eleanor L. Dulles, *The Wall: A Tragedy in Three Acts* (Columbia: University of South Carolina Press, 1972). A strong monograph on the Kennedy administration's relations with Africa is Richard B. Mahoney, *JFK: Ordeal in Africa* (New York: Oxford University Press, 1983); on Algeria there is Ronald J. Nurse, "Critic of Colonialism: JFK and Algerian Independence," *The Historian*, vol. 39 (February 1977), pp. 307–326o. Two recent studies focusing exclusively on Kennedy and Vietnam are Ralph B. Smith, *An International History of the Vietnam War: The Kennedy Strategy* (New York: St. Martin's Press, 1986) and William J. Rust, *Kennedy in Vietnam* (New York: Scribner's, 1985); see also Roger Hilsman, *To Move a Nation* (Garden City, N.Y.: Doubleday, 1967); Richard N. Goodwin, *Triumph or Tragedy, Reflections on Vietnam* (New York: Random House, 1966); and David Halberstam, *The Best and the Brightest* (New York: Random House, 1972). Glenn T. Seaborg has written *Kennedy and the Test-Ban Treaty* (Berkeley: University of California Press, 1983). Gerard T. Rice looks at *The Bold Experiment: JFK's Peace Corps* (Notre Dame: University of Notre Dame Press, 1986). Montague Kern et al. have written *The Kennedy Crises: The Press, the Presidency, and Foreign Policy* (Chapel Hill: University of North Carolina Press, 1983); for the press conferences there is *The Kennedy Presidential Press Conferences,* introduction by David Halberstam (E.M. Coleman Enterprises, 1978). On the Grand Alliance see Frank Costigliola, "The Failed Design: Kennedy,

De Gaulle and the Struggle for Europe," *Diplomatic History*, vol. 8 (Summer 1984), pp. 227–251. The Alliance for Progress is covered in Jerome Levinson and Juan de Onis, *The Alliance that Lost Its Way: A Critical Report on the Alliance for Progress* (New York: Quadrangle Books, 1970) and Harvey S. Perloff, *Alliance for Progress: A Social Invention in the Making* (Baltimore: The Johns Hopkins University Press, 1969). On Kennedy's relations with China see the article by Gordon Chang in the March 1988 *Journal of American History*.

The Cuban Missile crisis is a cottage industry in itself: Graham Alison, *Essence of Decision* (Boston: Little, Brown, 1971); Elie Abel, *The Missile Crisis* (Philadelphia: Lippincott, 1968); David Detzer, *The Brink* (New York: Thomas Y. Crowell, 1979); Herbert Dinerstein, *The Making of a Missile Crisis: October 1962* (Baltimore: The Johns Hopkins University Press, 1970); Abram Chayes, *The Cuban Missile Crisis* (New York: Oxford University Press, 1974). White House oral history tapes at the Kennedy Library in Dorchester, Massachusetts, include deliberations over the Cuban missiles. Essays on the crisis include Richard N. Lebow, "The Cuban Missile Crisis: Reading the Lessons Correctly," *Political Science Quarterly*, vol. 98, pp. 431–458, and a series of articles by Barton Bernstein that argues for Kennedy's culpability.

Domestic affairs under Kennedy have received considerably less attention than foreign. Like many other books on the civil rights movement, Carl Bauer's *John F. Kennedy and the Second Reconstruction* (New York: Columbia University Press, 1977) has sparked controversy. Harris Wofford's *Of Kennedys and Kings* (New York: Farrar, Straus, & Giroux, 1980) is an account by a participant, and Burke Marshall gives his important views in *Federalism and Civil Rights* (New York: Columbia University Press, 1964) See also Jim F. Heath's *John F. Kennedy and the Business Community* (Chicago: University of Chicago Press, 1969); Grant McConnell, *Steel and the Presidency, 1962* (New York: W. W. Norton 1963); James L. Sundquist, *Politics and Policy: The Eisenhower, Kennedy and Johnson Years* (Washington: Brookings Institution, 1968); Alan Shank, *Presidential Policy Leadership: Kennedy and Social Welfare* (Lanham, Md.: University Press of America, 1980); and Allen Matusow's New American Nation Series volume, *The Unraveling of America: A History of Liberalism in the 1960s* (New York: Harper & Row, 1984). Aida De Pace Donald's edited volume of essays is still important: *John F. Kennedy and the New Frontier* (New York: Hill and Wang, 1966); see also Edmund S. Ions, ed., *The Politics of John F. Kennedy* (New York: Barnes & Noble, 1967). There are at least four important articles on Kennedy's domestic actions or inaction: Robert E. Gilbert, "John F. Kennedy and Civil Rights for Black Americans," *Presidential Studies Quarterly,* vol. 12 (Summer 1982), pp. 386–399; John Hart, "Kennedy, Congress and Civil Rights," *Journal of American Studies,* vol. 13 (August 1979), pp. 165–178; Cynthia E. Harrison, "A 'New Frontier' for Women: The Public Policy of the Kennedy Administration," *Journal of American History,* vol. 67 (June 1980), pp. 630–46; and Carl Brauer, "Kennedy, Johnson and the War on Poverty," *Journal of American History,* vol. 69 (June 1982), pp. 98-119.

Miscellaneous works include David Burner and Thomas R. West, *The Torch Is Passed: The Kennedy Brothers and American Liberalism* (New York: Atheneum Publishers, 1984); Lewis Paper, *The Promise and the Performance: The Leadership of John F. Kennedy* (New York: Crown Publishers, 1975); John M. Logsdon, *The Decision to Go to the Moon: Project Apollo and the National Interest* (Cambridge, Mass.: M.I.T. Press, 1970); Ralph G. Martin, *JFK: A Hero of Our Times* (New York: Macmillan, 1983); John H. Davis, *The Kennedys* (New York: McGraw-Hill, 1984); Theodore H. White, *The Making of the President 1960* (New York: Atheneum Publishers, 1961); Nelson Polsby, ed., *The Modern Presidency* (New York: Random House, 1973); T. David et al., *The Presidential Election and Transition, 1960–1961* (Washington: Brookings Institution, 1961); the interesting and not uncritical campaign biography by James MacGregor Burns, *John Kennedy: A Political Profile* (New York:

Harcourt, Brace, 1960); Normal Mailer, *The Presidential Papers* (New York: Putnam, 1963); Lawrence H. Fuchs, *John F. Kennedy and American Catholicism* (New York: Meredith Press, 1967); Warren Cohen, *Dean Rusk* (Totowa, N.J.: Cooper Square Publishers, 1980); Henry Trewhitt, *McNamara: His Ordeal at the Pentagon* (New York: Harper & Row, 1971); Maxwell Taylor, *Swords and Plowshares* (New York: W. W. Norton, 1972); James David Barber, *The Presidential Character: Predicting Performance in the White House* (Englewood Cliffs, N.J.: Prentice-Hall, 1972); Tom Wicker, *JFK and LBJ* (New York: William Morrow, 1968); Arthur M. Schlesinger, Jr., *Kennedy or Nixon: Does It Make Any Difference?* (New York: Macmillan, 1960); Hugh Sidey, *John F. Kennedy, President* (New York: Atheneum, 1964); James Michener, *Report of the County Chairman* (New York: Random House, 1961); and Malcolm E. Smith, *Kennedy's 13 Great Mistakes in the White House* (Smithtown, N.Y.: National Forum of America, 1968). Books on the Kennedys to be avoided include the sentimental William Manchester, *One Brief Shining Moment* (Boston: Little, Brown, 1983) and the smarmy Peter Collier and David Horowitz, *The Kennedys: An American Drama* (New York: Summit Books, 1984). Supportive of the conspiracy theory of Kennedy's assassination is Michael L. Kurtz, *Crime of the Century: The Kennedy Assassination from a Historian's Perspective* (Knoxville: University of Tennessee Press, 1982) and Henry Hurt, *Reasonable Doubt* (New York: Holt, Rinehart & Winston, 1985); skeptical of conspiracies is Jean Davison, *Oswald's Game* (New York: W. W. Norton, 1983). For an accessible one-volume abridgment of the government's 1964 Warren Report see U.S. President's Commission on the Assassination of President John F. Kennedy, *Report of the Warren Commission on the Assassination of President Kennedy* (New York: McGraw-Hill, 1964). The *Report* (Washington, 1964) itself is based on twenty-six volumes of *Hearings Before the President's Commission on the Assassination of President Kennedy* (Washington, 1964). See also U.S. House of Representatives, Select Committee on the Assassination, *In-*

vestigation of the Assassination of Presidents, vol. 6 (Washington, 1979).

The most recent bibliography on JFK is Joan Newcomb, *John F. Kennedy* (Metuchen, N.J.: Scarecrow Press, 1977). Primary sources include U.S. Congress, *John Fitzgerald Kennedy: A Compilation of Statements and Speeches Made during His Service in the United States Senate and House of Representatives* (Washington, 1964) and President John F. Kennedy, *Public Papers of the President of the United States: John Fitzgerald Kennedy* (Washington, 1961, 1962, 1963, and 1964).

Index

DATE DUE

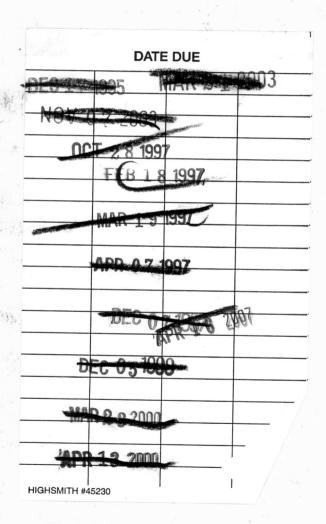